Madam Pres'
Thank you fr all
for do — & NEC
all the best
Sen Dolan
L=16-15

R - C - R

Also by Mark C. Bodanza

A Game That Forged Rivals
*How Competition Between Two New England High Schools
Created One of the Greatest Traditions in Football*

1933
Football at the Depth of the Great Depression

Make It Count
*The Life and Times of Basketball Great
JoJo White*

Resolve and Rescue
*The True Story of Frances Drake
and the Anti-Slavery Movement*

Ten Times a Champion
The Story of Basketball Legend Sam Jones

Leominster Chronicles
Tales from the Comb City

and

Rivals
More About the Fitchburg-Leominster Football Tradition

For me, Lou D'Allesandro is the flesh-and-blood embodiment of the greatest tradition in American democracy – the New Hampshire primary. When I was writing a book on the 2004 Democratic presidential race, I was continually puzzled as to why every contender was making a pilgrimage to the same seemingly ordinary home in Manchester. It was, of course, Lou and his wife Pat's home.

Since those innocent days, Lou has been my friend, my guide, my mentor and my favorite source on New Hampshire politics. No one knows the Granite State – and national Democratic politics – better. This spritely book honors Lou's remarkable career. Filled with colorful details that I didn't know about Lou's sporting and, yes, liberal Republican past, it is a treat to read and a wonderful tribute to my favorite person in politics.

Walter Shapiro, Columnist for *Roll Call,*
who has covered the last 10 New Hampshire primaries.
Author of *One-Car Caravan* and lecturer in political science at Yale.

∾

When a national reporter occasionally sounds knowledgeable about the upcoming, all-important New Hampshire presidential primary, it's a good bet that reporter has been listening to state senator Lou D'Allesandro who gives it to you – and to the candidate who has his support – straight from the shoulder.

In the unforgiving competition of New Hampshire politics, Lou has been winning elections for 45 years with a personal politics that has always been about people – their hopes, their families, their trials and their lives.

Lou D'Allesandro is much more than a good source; he is a good guy who takes his public service, but not himself, seriously. A savvy pol with a quick laugh, Lou has a terrific story well worth his telling and well worth your reading.

Mark Shields, PBS NewsHour
Columnist, Creators Syndicate

Lou D'Allesandro's story is the personification of what's become for many a bygone era of New Hampshire politics when it was unpretentious, instinctive and close to the people. Future politicos would do well to heed his advice for how to recapture that magic in the Granite State.

Kevin Landrigan, Senior Reporter,
New Hampshire Union Leader

~

Lou, I've had the honor and privilege of knowing "the skeleton of you" for about fifty years. I found the *Lou D'Allesandro the Lion of the New Hampshire Senate and Thoughts for Presidential Hopefuls* book interesting, educational and important. It certainly put a "lot of meat" on the D'Allesandro bones.

Seemingly you leave it up to the reader to ascertain whether you and your long political and governance prowess is the reason for the U.S. Presidential primary even being held in New Hampshire. This impression works for me.

Thomas "Satch" Sanders, former Boston Celtic
and member of the NBA Hall of Fame

~

I have known Lou D'Allesandro for more than 50 years. For twenty of those years he was my business partner in the Nelson-Sanders basketball camps.

He is one of the finest men I have ever known. I love him as a state senator and respect his ideas and what he stands for.

Don Nelson, former Boston Celtic
and NBA Coach

Lou D'Allesandro:

Lion of the New Hampshire Senate
and
Thoughts for Presidential Hopefuls

NORTH HILL PRESS

Leominster, Massachusetts

2018

Book and cover design by Robin Wrighton

Dust jacket photos of Lou D'Allesandro:
Front, Used by permission of the Concord Monitor
Inside, ©Tim Pierce /CC-BY-SA-3.0

ISBN: 978-0-9970144-2-6

Library of Congress Control Number: 2018939247

Bodanza, Mark C.
Lou D'Allesandro: Lion of the New Hampshire Senate
and Thoughts for Presidential Hopefuls

First Edition

1 2 3 4 5 6 7 8 9

Published by

NORTH HILL PRESS

36 School Street
Leominster, MA 01453

Northhillpress.com

Printed in Lowell, Massachusetts by King Printing Company

For information on publishing with North Hill Press,
or for special purchases contact: info@northhillpress.com

Dedication

To my family – my mother, who never saw her sons grow,
and to my immediate family: my wife, who rules the house,
and my children, who make life worth the struggle.

~ Lou

To my wife, Adele;
my children, Melissa, Kathryn, and Nicholas;
and my grandson, Brody, for all their love and support.

~ Mark

We Must Regain Our Moral Compass

I can remember the assassination of JFK in Dallas, the killing of Martin Luther King Jr., and the tragic murder of Robert Kennedy. These events altered the course of our nation's history, yes. But they also brought us together as Americans. In the past, when times got tough, we as a nation dug deep and worked together. We reaffirmed our values. We did not let difficulty or disagreement prevent us from moving forward and lifting one another up.

But today, it seems that we've lost that sense of resilience. Today, we let tragedy and uncertainty tear us apart. Day after day we hear of shootings all around our country. Many young children lose their lives and countless others are left to deal with the fallout from these tragedies. The resurgence of racism has come upon us, and there seems to be a growing disregard for caring for our neighbors. We live in a polarized society. We've lost faith in our political process. We lack the solutions-oriented leadership that once guided us through the toughest of times.

Have we as a nation lost our moral compass? At a time when our lives should be better, they are not. When we should be looking to our leaders for direction, we find nothing. I have lived in the best of times and have benefitted from hard work and the opportunities given to me. My work as a public servant has made me feel that I am part of trying to make things better. But I see today that the opportunities I had as a young man are less abundant than they once were, and that those whom we once looked to for direction are not the pillars of leadership they once were either.

In these trying times, we must demand more from our elected officials. Not only do they represent the face of our nation to the rest of the world, but they also set an example for us at home. We need leaders who will step up to bring us together, not exploit our differences for their own gain. We must hold accountable those who are responsible for conducting our politics. We must regain our moral compass and regain the positive place in the world which we have held for years.

We are a nation that has the will and the means to lead. The people must demand leadership that presents the best we can do. We all must do our part. That is what makes our nation work.

Dean of the New Hampshire State Senate

Senator Lou D'Allesandro represents Senate District 20, including the town of Goffstown and Wards 3, 4, 10 and 11 in Manchester, New Hampshire.

Table of Contents

Preface

At first glance, the subtitle of this book might seem solely related to New Hampshire's unique role in the United States presidential primary sweepstakes and Lou D'Allesandro's geographic share of Granite State democratic politics. Yet to think that would be wrong. If the admonition seems a bit inflated, one should first consider the other tenet on which the assertion is based.

Every political campaign will ultimately celebrate, true or not, a grassroots wave of support. But what is it or just how do you define the term exactly? It seems a bit like Justice Potter Stewart's famous quote in the obscenity case of *Jacobellis v. Ohio*. Admitting he "…could never succeed in intelligibly doing so," rather than define obscenity, he simply stated, "I know it when I see it."

The term "grassroots" may be much like that, more recognizable in its practice than a standard related in words. If any description exists, it is surely based in a candidate's relatability to the people. Every political organization, every candidate seeks it, but many will never truly know all the glory associated with a grassroots movement. A true grassroots phenomenon can never be created by a money-fueled political elite. No, real honest-to-goodness grassroots efforts are organic, the energy flows up from the people when it is merited. That reward is earned one person at a time through genuine relationships forged with the people.

If there was a course on forging authentic and sincere bonds with voters, Lou D'Allesandro could teach it. His brand of politics is based on listening to the concerns of his constituents and getting the job done. There is no pretense or elitist think tank guiding his every move, but only a desire to learn how he can help.

If that brand of street-level politics isn't fully adaptable to a run for president, all the gifts Lou employs on a daily basis would make any candidate a more favorable choice. At a visceral level, people know when they are getting snowed, whether it's by a candidate for a spot on the city council or the presidency. The art of caring in the world of politics happens one handshake, one look in the eye, one sympathetic listen at a time.

Lou D'Allesandro has been doing just that for nearly four decades. For all of those years, Pat, his wife of 56 years, has been by his side as Lou took an active role in the same community. His twenty-year tenure in the New Hampshire Senate proves it. His service in the senate, which gets tested every two years, is not so much the product of incumbency as it is a testament to the fact that he works as hard for his constituents today as the day he was first elected.

The first interview for this book took place at the kitchen table of the home he has lived in for nearly fifty years. The refrigerator is adorned with two decades' worth of photographs of presidential candidates. While we were sifting through a pile of newspapers clippings and letters, the phone rang. Lou fielded a call from a constituent concerned about a tax bill in the senate. Moments later there was another call and more constituent service. A few hours into the interview, Pat served us a delicious dinner of manicotti and meatballs. Before long there was a knock at the front door. A neighbor came to call about some proposed legislation in the senate. Lou greeted him warmly as the fellow apologized for the dinnertime interruption.

With Lou every exchange is the same; a friendly smile and an appreciation for those who trust him with the people's business. Whether it's some nice remarks at a Goffstown municipal meeting to celebrate the retirement of a longtime employee or a greeting at the hamburger bar across the street, the result is always the same. People leave thinking they just spoke with someone who cares. In an age of consultants, pollsters, targeted electronic canvasing and high-tech analytics, just maybe Lou D'Allesandro has an answer to the mountains of data – do more than make believe you care.

Author

CHAPTER I

When a President Calls

A loud cell phone ring interrupted the routine of the Manchester Water Board meeting one evening in 2007. Lou D'Allesandro, the Water Board president, reached into the pocket of his suit coat and answered the call. The voice on the other end quickly intoned, "Hi Lou, this is Bill Clinton." A surprised D'Allesandro replied, "How are you, Mr. President, how are things?" The former president got right to the point: "Lou I'm calling because I want you to support my wife in the primary."

D'Allesandro excused himself from the Water Board meeting, exiting to an anteroom, and the two men continued their conversation for ten minutes. To this day, Lou doesn't know how the former president got his cell phone number, and to be truthful, it doesn't much matter. On the Water Board agenda that evening was the review of a proposed rate hike, something the members were tussling over with Manchester's mayor, who opposed the increase. That of course had nothing at all to do with the former president's call. D'Allesandro would also say that his tenure on Manchester's Water Board had little to do with drawing Bill Clinton's notice that evening.

To label Lou D'Allesandro as a man of many pursuits and accomplishments would be an oversized understatement. Lou has had a career as varied as the White Mountains' skyline. But what attracted the former president's attention during that summer evening in 2007 was Lou's unique place in New Hampshire politics. It was not the first time the two men had talked. In fact, they had met a number of times before

2007 while Bill Clinton was either president or pursuing his own presidential campaigns. That night, the former chief executive was acting in a new capacity and his objective was quite clear – find a way to get his wife a win in the coveted New Hampshire presidential primary.

The state of New Hampshire is divided into twenty-four senatorial districts and most of them are held by Republicans.[1] In the summer of 2007, D'Allesandro, a Democratic incumbent, was the state senator for the 20th District. His district was, and still is, comprised of four of Manchester's twelve wards and the Town of Goffstown. Manchester, the state's most populous city, is divided among three state senatorial districts. D'Allesandro has held his 20th District seat since 1998, and the other two Manchester districts have not shown anything near that kind of allegiance to the Democratic Party.

If the foregoing seems like just a tangle of small-state politics, consider a few more realities. New Hampshire conducts the nation's first presidential primary every four years and has a law on the books that requires its primary to occur at least seven days before any "similar election" in any other state.[2] In eight of the New Hampshire presidential primaries conducted between 1960 and Bill Clinton's call to Senator D'Allesandro in 2007, the New Hampshire primary winner went on to secure the Democratic Party nomination for president. Only four times over that span did the New Hampshire winner fail to secure the nomination, and in two of the cases, the New Hampshire winner was the "favorite son" of a neighboring state. In 1972, Senator Muskie of Maine defeated the eventual winner, George McGovern, and twenty years later, Paul Tsongas, a Massachusetts senator, outpolled Bill Clinton before Clinton ultimately won the Democratic nomination and the presidency.[3] The peculiar place of New Hampshire in presidential politics is widely known.

Outside of the presidential primary arena, the normal flow of politics in the Granite State can often be routine. There are school board meetings, ball games, a bevy of community events, and plenty of constituent service opportunities sandwiched around senate sessions. "My constituent service is up close and personal," Lou says. "I go to the local gas station, the corner store and people's homes. I want to let my constituents know that I am there to help them." One quickly gets the sense that Lou has built a political career around a large network of relationships – genuine relationships. While the friendships Lou has forged pay admitted political dividends, it's evident that his motive in reaching out is pure. There are no empty stares or half-hearted handshakes from Lou. Moreover, we are talking about New Hampshire, a state that prides itself on authentic, straightforward politics. What other state in the nation could adopt, and keep, the motto, "Live Free or Die"? [4]

Senator D'Allesandro has a senate office in Concord; however, his district office is the kitchen table of his Manchester home. It is a unique setting for a man so often courted by some of the nation's most powerful Democrats. The pilgrimage of presidential hopefuls comes with each election cycle. There are phone calls, Christmas cards, letters and meetings at diners. Each time the primary season looms, Lou becomes the object of candidates eager for his endorsement and all that it means. Suitors for Lou's endorsement eventually find out that he is judicious in making the final determination as to who he will ultimately support. For Lou, his endorsement carries with it a responsibility. While he once noted, "I'm just a little guy from a little state," he knows that what he decides can have a significant impact on a presidential campaign. Every election is important, and each presidential election season seems to bring its own set of issues that challenge the nation. "It's important to the country. I've got to take my time and get it right."

A reflective Lou D'Allesandro collects his thoughts and figuratively pinches himself. Sometimes it all seems a bit surreal. How did he get to this point, not just as a player in the first-in-the-nation primary, but also all the other achievements and careers he has collected along the journey? He thinks about his humble beginnings, growing up and the trials and tribulations that went along with that. He wonders what some of his grammar school teachers would say about how he turned out, as it's likely a few would have had a lesser prophecy. Could anyone have predicted any of it? Lou's story is an American story in every way that the well-known cliché suggests. But at the same time, Lou's story is unique, with its own set of twists and turns. There is great value in its telling.

CHAPTER 2

Youthful Challenges

Lou D'Allesandro's earliest memory is an unsettling one. At the time, Lou was two years old and living with his family in their East Boston apartment building. On March 17, 1941, a day on which Bostonians not only paid homage to St. Patrick but celebrated Evacuation Day (the dislodging of British troops from Boston in 1776), calamity struck.[1] Lou was awakened in the early morning hours by his father and the firemen who were evacuating the family's apartment house, then fully engulfed in flames. The *Boston Globe* captured the ordeal. "Forced to flee through smoke-filled hallways were Mr. and Mrs. Louis D'Allesandro and their three young children, Victor, 6; Louis, 4; Paul; six months, and two sisters of Mrs. D'Allesandro, Julia and Edith Pinpaso." (The *Globe* was in error as to Lou's age at the time of the fire, two-and-a-half, as well as his oldest brother's name, which was Richard.)[2]

While the D'Allesandro family escaped from the third floor uninjured, other occupants of the house were not as fortunate. The charred body of John McClinchey, a second-floor tenant, was recovered from the ruins by firemen at 3:45 AM. Another second-floor tenant was badly hurt. According to the *Globe*, "one woman, the wife of a doctor (Mrs. Bianco), was seriously injured when she was forced to jump almost 30 feet from the rear piazza of her home and nine other persons were forced to flee to safety early this morning when a two-alarm fire swept a three-story dwelling at 40 Gladstone Street, East Boston. Damage was estimated at $10,000."[3]

While the D'Allesandro family was blessed to have their lives, the fire would have consequences that lasted long after the flames were extinguished.

The D'Allesandros would have to break up and establish separate living arrangements while the family recovered from the financial and property losses caused by the fire. Lou went to live with a maternal aunt, Irene Grygiel in Cambridge. He recalls those days away from his parents that were made much more tolerable by the care he received from his aunt. "Mother had a warm relationship with her sisters; I was treated well by Aunt Irene and Uncle Eddie." The temporary living arrangement lasted a number of months until Lou Sr. purchased a new two-family apartment house in the Orient Heights section of Boston at 102 Barnes Avenue. The family was reunited, including Mrs. D'Allesandro's sisters. There they spent the war years, struggling like all Americans to cope with challenges large and small. Lou attended St. Lazarus, a parochial grammar school nearby.

Only months after America's victory in World War II was complete with the signing of a peace treaty with Japan, the D'Allesandro family suffered another tragedy. This one was far more devastating than the fire five years before. In January of 1946, Lou's mother, Marion, died as a result of the complications of an ectopic pregnancy. She left behind her husband and sons, including two-year-old Henry, who had been born in 1941 after the fire. Marion's death caused an upheaval. "It left a gaping hole," Lou laments. "Mother was the heart and soul of the house." More than seventy years later, he describes his mother with great reverence and warmth. "She was so loving and a woman of great charity. She would take people off the street and feed them." He recalls her working at Schrafft's, a candy factory in the Sullivan Square section of Charlestown, Massachusetts.[4] "She used to bring home the seconds and take them to the convent for the nuns." Lou candidly notes, "My father was no piece of cake. My mother was a very special woman." Lou pauses and reflects for a moment, "You know they didn't take a lot of pictures in those days. I have only one picture of her."

That solitary photographic image is accompanied by countless other visions that reside warmly in Lou's mind. It isn't difficult to comprehend that much of Lou's penchant for public service comes from an ideal ingrained many decades ago by a mother who understood the virtue of serving other human beings. Her absence left a seven-year-old boy and his brothers to overcome many obstacles. "You are in a confused state," Lou observes. "My maternal grandmother and aunts moved in to help out. But things were not going to be the same."

Lou's father operated Crown Burners, a manufacturer and installer of oil heating equipment on Meridian Street in Boston. Lou Sr. wasn't around the house much. When he wasn't working, he was attending to a full social calendar. Lou recalls, "We didn't see much of him. He was a busy and very social guy." The elder Lou had his lady friends and soon strains developed in the household. Marion's family did not approve of Lou's new friends, and they let him know it. Lou and his younger brother Paul were sent to boarding school. They left St. Lazarus and entered the Academy of the Assumption in Wellesley, Massachusetts. It was there that Lou spent the third grade. He didn't like it. He felt isolated from the family. While his younger brother Paul was on campus, he lamented never getting to see his other brothers, especially his older brother Richard.

With tensions between the family members unabated, Lou Sr. sold the East Boston house and moved to Newton for a short time. A year later they moved again, this time to Medford. According to Lou, "The passing of my mother caused a family rift that never healed." With the purchase of the Medford home, Lou and his brother Paul changed schools again.

This time, the boys entered St. Joseph's Grammar School. Both of Lou's parents were of Italian ancestry. His mother's family, the Viscomis, were from Catanzaro, the capital of Italy's Calabria province. His paternal grandparents emigrated from Avellino. While the family lived in the Italian section of Medford, there was no Italian Catholic church in that city. St. Joseph's was an Irish parish. It was the first time Lou experienced prejudice. He remembers walking to church on Sundays with his brother Paul. The two have always been close and remain so today. Attending church was just one of the things they did together. On one particular Sunday, a resident they passed sneered, "Why don't you guineas go to your own church?" Lou's experiences in the parish school were not much more positive.

"We had a nun named Sister Nathaniel," Lou recalls with a grin. "We called her Nathan Hale." One might imagine that her intelligence-gathering didn't have the same catastrophic end result as that of her namesake. The Revolutionary War aside, the nun didn't mince words with Lou. She told him, "I don't see you ever getting out of the eighth grade." "My deportment was low," admits Lou. He was required to regularly attend meetings at the rectory to receive his report card, and that wasn't a good thing. At home, Lou's dad had remarried. Lou described his relationship with his stepmother Edna as "arm's-length." Before he was done, Lou's dad would marry two more times. He survived Edna, divorced his third wife Julia, and predeceased wife four Alice.

If Lou took anything away from his formative years with his dad, it might be an ease with people. When he was an adolescent that quality was not always something that was constructively channeled. Like most young people he was finding his way – forging an identity. In those grammar school days, Lou describes himself as a "semi-wise guy, on the cusp." It was probably sports that kept him from going over the edge. His older brother Richard was a talented football player and Lou wanted to emulate him. Richard played the tackle position – both ways – and made the all-scholastic team at Medford High School. The high school star got plenty of favorable newspaper ink and eventually the notoriety earned him a football scholarship to Brandeis University. The younger brother tried his best to keep up and was a regular participant in pick-up football and basketball games on neighborhood fields and courts. "It kept us going," noted Lou. Sports would have a definite impact on his future. It was what kept him on the straight and narrow and would have more than short-term consequences alone. In spite of Sister Nathaniel's dour prediction, Lou graduated from St. Joseph's Grammar School.

The next stop on Lou D'Allesandro's educational journey took him a thousand miles south to Gainesville, Georgia. There he entered the Riverside Military Academy, which catered to young men in grades 7-12. Once again, his younger brother Paul went with him. "Dad was a widower with four boys and it was difficult for his new wife to cope," Lou notes. "It didn't make sense to send the oldest boy, Richard, or the youngest, Henry, away. given their respective ages." So once again, Lou and Paul were the ones that got shipped off. As Lou admits, "A military academy was under consideration because I was a little wild and hard to handle at school."

"The change came out of the blue," says Lou. "I certainly had many thoughts at the time, primarily – what was it all about?" It was his dad's decision and Lou knew there no going back on it. It was something he simply had to accept. The brothers were dressed in jackets with a tag affixed: "Deliver to Riverside Military in Gainesville." Unfortunately for the brothers, uncertainty developed as to their proper destination and the boys were sent on their way to Gainesville, *Florida.* The young travelers were at the Atlanta Airport when the possibility of an error was discovered, A great deal of confusion ensued while the bewildered boys hoped for someone to come up with a definitive decision. Fortunately, another traveler who was also headed to the academy overheard the conversation and directed Lou and Paul to the proper place.

Confusion was not the only thing that Lou experienced upon his arrival in Atlanta. In that Southern airport Lou first witnessed segregated facilities. "We arrived at the Atlanta Airport and for the first time in my life I saw 'black only' and 'white only' bathrooms and water fountains. I had never seen anything like it before and I wondered what it was all about." Just as impactful to Lou was another observation that he made soon after his arrival in the South. "I was amazed that when a black person saw me, he would cross to the other side so as not to be in my way."

The boys' only contact with black Americans at the academy was the workers employed to complete manual tasks. Students at the academy, which was established in 1907, were from all over the country but almost all were from wealthy families.[5] Some of the cadets at Riverside were international students, primarily from South America and Mexico. The student body represented a broad cross-section of cultures from different parts of the United States and abroad. Lou and Paul had each other to help with the adjustment to life at a military academy, a far cry from grammar school in Medford, Massachusetts. Lou entered Riverside as a ninth grader and would spend two years at the school.

A big part of student life at Riverside was sports. This was just fine with Lou because it was his interest in sports that had helped ground him before he was packed up and sent south. Lou recalls, "My love of sports made life away from home bearable." Not surprisingly, football was the premier sport at a school that was keen on emphasizing manly virtues. Lou already had a deep affection for football and the sport was an effective way for him to find acceptance with the student body.

Lou's football talents were being noticed. His exposure to coaching fundamentals and an organized structure was improving his game. His football participation was not without risk however. During one game, Lou dislocated his hip. In pain, his transportation to the hospital was in the bed of a pickup truck. Paul stayed by his older brother's side on the way to the emergency room. The doctors put Lou's hip back in place and he got a ride back to campus in the same pickup truck.

Fortunately, the body healed and the transplanted football player was able to return to the gridiron again. That was a good thing, something that would pay future dividends. Not unlike his older brother, Lou would discover that his ability as an imposing lineman would open a few educational doors. Those opportunities would not only have an impact on his schooling but help direct his future journey in other ways as well.

CHAPTER 3

Opportunity on the Gridiron

n August of 1954, Lou found himself in pre-season football workouts at Worcester Academy. The private school, which took its name from its location in Massachusetts' second-largest city, educated day and boarding school students from grade nine through twelve. The school also "finished" postgraduate students, often talented high school athletes, being prepped for college careers.[1] Like Riverside, the choice of Worcester Academy had little to do with Lou. The decision was made by Lou's father after hearing from Henry Hormel, who was a recruiter for the school. Hormel, also the assistant headmaster at Medford High, was well-acquainted with the athletic talent of the D'Allesandro boys, both Lou and his older brother Richard.

The Worcester Academy wasn't the only school considered for Lou. His older brother's coaches at Medford High had their own suggestions. Head coach John Pryor pushed his alma mater, the Milford School of Connecticut, and Torbert Macdonald, Medford's assistant football coach, tried without success to get Lou into Phillips Andover. Macdonald was a Harvard University graduate who had a rather famous roommate at the school, John F. Kennedy. Macdonald, who was also a lawyer, was elected to congress the same year Lou entered Worcester Academy.

Whatever the school choice for Lou and Paul, living at home wasn't really an option for the boys anyways. Their stepmother Edna had little interest in raising stepsons and Lou Sr. saw no value in his sons spending their idle time in Medford Square. So, Lou enrolled as a Hilltopper for his junior year. His brother Paul was admitted to the school as a freshman.

Today, Lou would agree that loitering by the pool hall in Medford probably wasn't a very good idea. He recalls standing on a corner and giving the "Italian salute" (thumb to the nose with a waving hand) to a police officer in a passing squad car. The cop made a quick U-turn and went to grab Lou for a trip to the station. Lou remembers, "Most of the cops were Irish, and in the 1950s a trip to the station, especially for guys like us (Italians), meant a good beating." Fortunately for Lou, his older brother Richard was standing nearby and saw the commotion. Richard was an imposing young man, "intimidating," according to his younger brother. "He told the cop, you're not taking my brother anywhere," remembers Lou, and the crisis was averted.

For Lou, attending Worcester Academy was an improvement over his time at the military academy in Georgia. "At least it was better because people could come and see us play [football] and we could go home once in a while." Perched atop one of Worcester's hills, it was one of the oldest private schools of its type in the country. Started in 1834, Worcester Academy had once enjoyed a preeminent reputation, but by the time Lou and Paul arrived there, the place had fallen on hard times. The facilities were deteriorating and the school was in need of students. The school's circumstances were in part the reason for a growing emphasis on attracting postgraduate students in autumn 1954.

Lou's prowess on the gridiron saved his father tuition dollars. The arrangement was straightforward: Lou played football and worked in the dining hall, and in turn his tuition payment was reduced. Playing football was not a chore for D'Allesandro. The sport wouldn't be his biggest adjustment to life at Worcester Academy, but it would be his first experience at the preparatory school. During the last days of August, Lou and his teammates sweated in the late summer warmth. While the boys drilled and trained, Hurricane Carol struck New England. The storm, which caused thirty-six deaths in the New England states and toppled the steeple of the Old North Church in Boston, forced the football team from the field.[2] The boys hunkered down in one of the campus buildings and rode out the storm. The tornado that had devastated the City of Worcester just a year before couldn't have been too far from the mind of head coach Al Alpena when he directed his squad to safety. Hurricane Carol didn't damage the school, but the $462 million dollars in total destruction it caused to the East Coast was, at the time, the costliest storm that had ever struck the New England states.[3]

When the team was able to return to the field, Coach Alpena installed his offense. It was a straight T formation with an unbalanced line, modeled after a system run by Michigan State. Lou remembers the coach, "He was a detail guy, creative, and tough, very tough, and very high-strung emotionally." With all the postgrads on the team, Lou was one of the few true juniors on the squad. He was tapped to be a starting tight end and defensive end. Lou's roommate, also a Medford boy, was named starting quarterback. "We had a good season," notes Lou. "The team was close and the older guys were good athletes." The football team finished its season 4-2-1.

Without the slightest hesitation, the game that stands out in Lou's mind after all those years is the tie. The team traveled to Phillips Andover Academy in Andover, Massachusetts. Lou remembers being surprised by the beauty of the campus there. "I was awestruck, really." No one expected the game on the field to be any less disparate than the quality of the two campuses; that is, except for the young men from Worcester. "Tying Phillips Andover was a big accomplishment," recalls D'Allesandro. "We surprised a lot of people, set a tone." It didn't take long for that assessment to be proved as other schools started dropping Worcester Academy from their schedule.

Lou had good success on the football field his first season at the Academy. He remembers putting in a solid effort in a game against Dean Junior College. The solid tight end caught a pass on a crossing pattern. As he went over the middle and grabbed the spiral, he got whacked hard. When he went to the sideline, his coach took a look at his bloodied face, framed by a leather helmet during days when a facemask was a pretty rare option. The coach did a double take. "We got to get you a facemask," he barked. Lou completed the season as he started it – with a facemask-less helmet.

If Lou had held a love for the game for some time, his junior year certainly cemented it. One thing that made the gridiron even more appealing at Worcester Academy was the opportunity to play in front of his dad and older brother Richard. Lou Sr. was not effusive in his praise; it was just the way he was. But it was evident to Lou that his dad loved the game too and that he was proud of his son. Apparently, Lou made a favorable impression on his teammates as well. The squad elected D'Allesandro as captain of the football team for 1955, his senior year.

The adjustment to academics would not come as easily as the athletic experience. Still, the extra effort required may have made the progress Lou achieved in that realm all the more rewarding. "We [Lou and Paul] had to find our way. I think it made us tougher, mentally and physically tougher." The faculty at Worcester Academy made a great difference in Lou's future. A number of instructors lived on the campus. The classes were small and when Lou didn't adapt initially, he got lots of attention and tutoring.

He remembers Richard Johnson, the geometry teacher, well. "We called him Mr. Peepers; he was a bit eccentric, but a very kind guy. He had a young family that lived on the campus. He could understand students." In Lou's graduation yearbook, under the photo of the bespectacled Johnson, appears the following inscription, "30-60 you should be able to do anything." Johnson's quip was a reference to Lou's grade progress, perhaps not stellar in result, but solid in progress. The next instructor in the yearbook may have summed it up best. His name was Robert J. Lusena, and he just happens to have been the author's uncle. Lusena wrote, "Best of luck to you, Lou, keep playing hard and work as hard."[4]

Lou's academic progress was steady but his socialization in school was punctuated by a few altercations. He wasn't one to look for trouble, but he didn't look away from it either. He had a scrap with his roommate when they first bunked together, but that settled down and the two became friends. Another student picked a fight with him in Spanish class. "I didn't back down," recalls Lou. "Life made me tough and I had my older brother Richard as an example." Despite a few bumps in the road, Lou made a solid start at the school. He returned home to Medford for the summer with a sense he had accomplished a good deal both academically and on the football field. He had forged some solid friendships and was popular.

Jobs kept Lou occupied during the summer school break. In the summer of 1955, Americans were in the midst of discovering a number of new consumer trends and a changing popular culture. The first McDonald's restaurant opened, and Coca-Cola debuted the packaging of its all-American beverage in cans.[5] Perhaps the most notable beginning that summer was the opening of Disneyland in Anaheim, California, on July 17.[6] By the fall, Walt Disney introduced the transformative Mickey Mouse Club on the ABC television network.[7] More mature audiences could tune their televisions to the first episodes of the western, *Gunsmoke*, or the quiz show, *The 64,000 Question*. Adolescents like Lou were entertained by the strains of evolving rock and roll with stars like Elvis Presley, Bill Haley and the Comets, and Chuck Berry.[8]

Initially, D'Allesandro worked for his dad that summer but he eventually landed a job with Boston's Metropolitan District Commission (MDC) on the highway crew. The work involved maintaining the Stone Zoo and mowing lawns along the Charles River basin on Storrow Drive. The MDC also operated a pool just across from Massachusetts General Hospital in the same area where Lou was mowing grass. He spent some of his time as an MDC lifeguard. The pool may have provided the most dramatic moments of his summer. One warm afternoon, an MDC employee named Brown decided to cool off in the pool. Unfortunately, the fellow got into trouble right away and was drowning. The crisis got Lou's attention quickly and he dove in after the flailing Brown. Lou pulled the man out of the water and saved his life. The event was a clear punctuation to what had otherwise been an ordinary schoolboy summer.

As the last days of August hinted at the coming of autumn, Lou's thoughts turned to football. His senior season at Worcester Academy would be different in a number of ways. Not only was he stepping into the role of captain, but the 1955 team had a new head coach. John Pietro stepped into a long line of accomplished football mentors at a school that boasts, in recent times, two NFL head coaches, Joe Philbin (Miami Dolphins) and Mike Sherman (Green Bay Packers).[9] Pietro was a Brown University graduate where he played guard on the football team. He was selected by the Cleveland Browns with the 336th pick in the 1952 NFL draft.[10]

There was another significant distinction that set the 1955 season apart. The school recruited more than twenty-five postgraduate students and many of them ended up on the football team. The senior class numbered a record 125 students. The competition for starting roles and playing time on the football team was keen. The postgrads in particular were looking to showcase their talents for college scholarships and those heightened ambitions caused tensions. Some of the players resented Lou's role as captain. Lou had a new roommate, Paul Cancro, who was also a solid contributor on the team. An undercurrent of animosity was directed toward Lou and Cancro. Finally, emotions bubbled to the surface and a minor fight occurred in the dormitories. It was a revolt of sorts. Worse than the scrap were the feelings that haunted Lou in the aftermath.

His relationship with many of the players was never the same. "It was a very distracting time," recalls Lou. "I got my first real taste of animosity and jealousy." Coach Pietro never interceded in the whole muddle. He did his best to cater to the older players who were clamoring for playing time. Lou maintained his starting roles on offense and defense and, despite the rancor; the team had a solid season, losing only one of its six games. The only blemish came at the hands of the Tufts University freshman team, 21-14.[11]

As his final football season at the Academy faded, Lou turned his attention to college. Coach Pietro was pushing his alma mater, but Lou's SAT scores weren't high enough for Brown. D'Allesandro applied to three other colleges: the University of Colorado, Boston University, and the University of New Hampshire. He was accepted at all three schools. Lou decided on the Colorado Buffaloes. The college awarded him a full NCAA scholarship, which included tuition, room and board, a $15-per-month stipend, and a voucher for plane trips to visit home.

The boy from Medford was on his way to Boulder. His graduation yearbook, the 1956 *Towers*, is filled with inscriptions lauding his football talent and leadership on the field. Looking back today, and between the faded lines scrawled with fountain pens, another, more subtle theme emerges. The well-wishes of classmates describe a young man who was well-liked, not just for his football skills, but also for his approachable, engaging personality. In retrospect, it's not hard to see that even then, the seeds of Lou's future successes were already planted.

CHAPTER 4

College Life from Colorado to New Hampshire

I n late August 1956, Lou found himself at the intersection of a cheerful summer and a flight to Boulder. A sweetheart in Medford was his frequent companion that summer. When he wasn't working at the MDC, the two were making the most of the warm days of July and August. Lou borrowed his uncle's Hudson Hornet so the couple could make trips to Hampton Beach in New Hampshire. They also took shorter rides down Route 16 to a club at Revere Beach called Frolics. Lou Sr. knew the owner of the club and was a patron himself. The place was a destination of sorts and featured some notable acts playing the sort of music that could set a tone for its guests. Jerry Vale is one example of the caliber of talent that performed there. "I was a Frank Sinatra lover and I really enjoyed the place," remembers Lou. But if there was a song that stood out to him that summer, it may have been "Teach Me Tonight" by the DeCastro Sisters. They were a Latin-flavored trio that sang Lou's song of summer to a number two spot on the charts in 1954.[1] While Peggy, Cherie, and Babette crooned their song's first line, "Did you say I've got a lot to learn…" Lou was saying his goodbyes to his girlfriend and hopping a plane to the University of Colorado.

It was not Lou's first trip to Boulder. He had visited the university on a recruiting trip earlier in the year. He got first-class treatment from the moment he stepped on the plane for the initial trip that spring. The stewardess, (the term flight attendant was still decades away from use) who knew he was a football recruit, treated Lou with great kindness. It was almost as if she was part of the welcome wagon. On campus he was accompanied by head coach Dallas Ward and Will Walls, the school's recruiter on his tour. Walls later became the head of player personnel for the Dallas Texans, forerunner of the Kansas City Chiefs.[2] "They took me to the school, the stadium and later a country club," recalls Lou. "Everything was bigger than life. I thought that I could play there, that I could do well. I remember feeling that I must have been a good player if someone wanted me."

The second trip to Boulder was a bit more down-to-earth, however. The niceties were over. It wasn't the football that Lou was worried about. Lou had a quiet confidence in his abilities on the gridiron. In any event, freshmen couldn't play varsity football in those days. It was the separation from home and his girlfriend that weighed on him at times. Other than the occasional homesickness, the assimilation went well. "All of the scholarship guys lived together in the dorm," Lou notes. "I got friendly with a number of the varsity players and they liked me." D'Allesandro felt validated by some pretty good "Big 7" talent. (The conference's name was changed to the "Big 8" in 1960).[3] Those upperclassmen included John Wooten, a guard who went on to play for the Cleveland Browns; end Frank Clarke, who played for the Dallas Cowboys; and Boyd Dowler, an end who had a professional career with the Green Bay Packers.[4]

Colorado gave Lou a sense of what big-time football was all about. The freshman football players had to park cars at the stadium for games. "It was the first time I saw fans arrive for a game by helicopter," notes D'Allesandro. "It was also the first time I came into contact with Texans. I came to realize just how big football was in Texas." It was a good season for the Colorado Buffaloes. While the team lost the conference championship to its rival Oklahoma, Colorado secured the conference's Orange Bowl bid since the conference champion could not be awarded the Orange Bowl game two years in a row.[5]

Lou's personal football season was successful, too. The Colorado freshman team only played two games but the Medford gridder contributed solid efforts in both encounters. Despite all that was going right on the football field, Lou still wasn't sold on the notion of staying in Colorado. Given the distance from home, he didn't envision his family attending games. When the Thanksgiving holiday came, it was not practical for him to go home and celebrate with his family. While the family of a classmate from Colorado Springs graciously opened their home to him, it just wasn't the same. Then of course, there was the girl. She called him once a week, which was more than enough to serve as a reminder of their lengthening separation.

Finally, the first semester ended, and Lou went east to celebrate the holidays. He never returned to Boulder. A female friend from Colorado who was aware of his decision wrote to him, "How do you write a letter to a person you know you will never see again?" In December 1956, communication like we have come to know today was still in the distant future. Long-distance phone calls were a luxury and the speed of internet-age exchanges did not exist. Lou is a sentimental guy and after all these years he still remembers that solitary letter from so long ago.

Lou's father wasn't pleased with his decision. Leaving Colorado meant the loss of an NCAA scholarship and uncertainty as to his son's future education. There was also the matter of Edna. Having Lou and his younger brother Paul around the house wasn't exactly going to please her, so the father had another issue to deal with. Lou never even had a key to the house as long as Edna was ruling the roost. For Lou the decision was firm, but that didn't stop him from wondering what a career in big-time college football would have meant. During his semester off, he flirted with the notion of enrolling at the University of Miami. He had a chance to visit the school when the family spent the Christmas holiday at a home Lou Sr. had built on land owned by Edna's mother in Florida. Lou didn't care for the trip or the school. About the only pleasant thing coming out of the Florida trip was a chance to see some of the Colorado guys who had just beaten Clemson in the Orange Bowl.

After passing on the University of Miami, it was effectively decided that Lou would attend college much closer to home. Given the dearth of big-time college football programs in New England, Lou would not get to compete on the highest level. "I never got a chance to test myself on the football field," Lou notes. It doesn't register as a full-scale regret with him today, something more akin to a wonder. Life's journey presents a number of paths and options, and Lou was on the precipice of making some impactful decisions.

What would have been Lou's spring semester of 1957 was spent working in his dad's heating business, just as President Eisenhower was commissioning a study to determine if oil imports were endangering the nation's security.[6] Lou considered two of the schools where he originally applied, Boston University and the University of New Hampshire (UNH), for the fall of 1957. Boston University wasn't his first choice of the two schools. Besides, he would be footing the bill and UNH was less expensive. Beyond finances, the more rural location of UNH appealed to him. "I had an attachment to New England," observes Lou. "Besides, I would be close to Paul attending school in New England. The decision to attend the University of New Hampshire altered my whole life."

But before he could make plans to move to the Durham campus, Lou had to make the necessary financial arrangements. That meant hustling for the summer. UNH didn't pay the football money Colorado did and transfer students weren't eligible to receive any money, however meager. So while Elvis Presley hit his stride with the film *Jailhouse Rock* and the ABC television network debuted its show *American Bandstand*, Lou went to work.[7] Hustling meant a second job. He kept his day job working for his dad's company and took up a second job at Wonderland, a greyhound racing park in Revere, Massachusetts. His father owned dogs that raced there, and Lou not only earned some extra money but got an education that doesn't appear on a college syllabus.

His summer job at Wonderland involved arriving promptly at 5:00 PM so he could weigh all the dogs for the night's card. For this chore he was paid an extra $100 for the season. His regular calling at the track was as a "lead out boy." He was one of the fellows who paraded the dogs before the crowd before installing the canine sprinters in the starting apparatus for their unfruitful chase after the mechanical rabbit. The crowds were big in those days and the gambling spirited. Lou learned how to gamble that summer. At the same time, he observed the unique blend of trouble that gambling, liquor and women can produce.

His own romantic relationship, which had been at least partially responsible for drawing him home, had played out. It was slightly awkward, since Lou's girlfriend babysat for Lou's older brother Richard and his wife. A friendship had developed between Lou's former girlfriend and the couple. Nevertheless, Lou was moving on from the relationship and to a new start in Durham. He earned enough money to pay for his first year there, which he supplemented with a "work-study" job in the cafeteria, a bargain freshman meal ticket and dormitory housing. His initial impressions of UNH were good. He settled into the dorm, his classes and a role on the football team.

With the transfer of his credits from Colorado, Lou was a second-semester freshman. As a result, his preclusion from varsity football remained. Says Lou, "I didn't want to flatter myself, but I was better than most of the varsity football players." It didn't take him long to realize he wasn't at Colorado. There was no weight room and the training facilities were sparse. The stadium was modest and the coaching staff and methods did not compare with football as it was played at the Big 7 schools. Still, none of this was a tremendous surprise to Lou; he had made a conscious choice. He spent his first football season at the school working out with varsity and playing on the scout team. The team was coached by a couple of fellows with unusual names, Chief Boston and his assistant "Whoops Snively." The squad wasn't very good that first year. UNH played in the Yankee Conference and the conference competition was improving. The Wildcats were going to have to make future strides to keep pace.

Lou's rough and tumble was not limited to the football field that fall. He took up his duties on the lunch line with the cafeteria staff. When an insolent student made a disrespectful remark about the appearance of a lady staff member, Lou jumped over the counter and exacted some immediate justice. The unhesitating action won Lou great favor with the cafeteria staff. It was something they never forgot. Later those same ladies helped in Lou's campaigns and joined with him in sponsoring a bill, The School Feeding and Nutrition Act.

The most notable thing that happened that fall however, was meeting Patricia Morganstern, his future wife. Their first encounter was in a sociology class. Lou formed some initial impressions. "I thought she was smart, quiet and not bad-looking. I always fell for a woman that wore glasses." The future couple did not have the most auspicious of starts. Lou's first appeal was cerebral. He asked Patricia to help him out with some of his classes. If romance was in the air, it was greatly impeded, at least in the early stages, by the fact that they both had other conquests on their mind. Circumstances changed and some people on campus started to observe the couple's growing affinity for each other. Pat's dormitory friends playfully admonished Patricia to "be careful." The smitten freshman scored his first date at the Winter Carnival, one of the school's biggest social events. "We had our ups and downs," says Lou. "We finally started to 'go steady' and the rest is history."

For a lot of reasons, not the least of which was Patricia Morganstern, Lou wrapped up his first year at UNH with a different perspective. If the school year was marked by change, summer employment was not. Once again, he hustled at his dad's company by day and at the dog track evenings. When he could get some time off he'd borrow a car for a trip up Route 93 to visit Patricia in Manchester. When a car wasn't available, Lou could hop a train from Boston. A summer of activity passed by quickly and before long, it was time for his first real introduction to Wildcat football.

Players needed an invitation to football camp and there wasn't any real doubt that Lou would receive his. During a warm August week in 1958, Lou worked his way to a starting position on the Wildcat Football Team. Camp was austere. There wasn't even an official school source of meals for the players since the kitchen didn't open until the rest of the students arrived on campus. The team was fed by boosters who lived nearby or fed at a fraternity house. The team was only slightly better than the UNH contingent from the prior season.

Chief Boston was used to coaching former GIs back from war. The men were pushed hard, and the object was simple: hit the line hard, over and over again. Boston never made the adjustment to more modern technique. The UNH playbook wasn't long on passing, or plays dependent on deceptive, speedy execution. Boston was a good guy, just set in his ways. Despite that, Lou admits, "I can't knock it, it was a great experience. I became very well known in town, and well regarded." Lou was a bona fide star at UNH and he helped the school fill its stadium. It wasn't Colorado, but the Wildcats and Durham appreciated him.

During his second year at UNH, Lou pledged Phi Kapa Theta, a Catholic fraternity at the school, as freshmen couldn't pledge fraternities. The frat house, nicknamed the "Green Latrine" for its exterior color and interior housekeeping, was the party venue on campus. At that time, alcohol was not sold in Durham, so the frat houses held a monopoly on the best parties. "Our fraternity was the social gathering place on campus," notes Lou. "We were regular guys who liked fun and were good practical jokers." Lou especially enjoyed the rhythm and blues bands that the Green Latrine featured. In particular, he remembers an act called the "Fuzzies." As the Latrine swayed to Jackie Wilson, the Coasters or the Platters, Lou settled into his room. His "room" was a portion of the front porch, a little drafty, and with no heat. If the unadorned accommodations were a bit harsh, it was good preparation for his next chapter. Lou made an important decision and joined the Marines' Platoon Leaders program for the summer. The Cold War was a reality of the times and Lou felt it was time to make a contribution.

US-Soviet relations continued to dominate the national conversation in 1959, but there were some signs of improvement. The Soviets opened a technology and culture exhibition in New York on June 29 and Vice President Nixon visited Moscow later that summer when the U.S. opened a similar exhibition there.[8] While the dignitaries were touting the advances of their societies, the new recruit was sweating at Quantico. "It was demanding mentally and physically," D'Allesandro remembers. "It was really, really tough – a unique experience. It called upon you to demonstrate leadership."

Lou thought the military would be a good career. Successful candidates were commissioned as a Marine Corps Second Lieutenant upon college graduation. Not all the students who joined made it. "Half of the college students washed out," observed Lou. One of Lou's roommates at Quantico didn't make it. It is a particularly disturbing memory. Distraught at his failure, the young man tried to take his own life by slitting his throat. Those who persevered were changed. Long days that started with forced marches and hours of combat training had a marked impact on the young recruits, and Lou went back to UNH with a new perspective.

Lou declared himself a history major during the fall semester of 1959. "I became friendly with the department head and he was a great mentor. I was doing well academically." The Marine Corps training was all the preparation he needed for the new football season. "It was a good year all around," Lou says with a smile. He was targeted with more passes on the gridiron and the Wildcats had a good deal of success.

In between the rigors of academics and football, as well as time spent with Patricia, Lou still had to earn some expense money. In the 1959-60 academic year, that meant unloading one-hundred-pound sacks of flour and salt at a rail siding for a large commercial bakery in Dover. When Lou wasn't feeding the bakery its raw materials, he was cleaning the seating area and floors of the UNH field house for sixty cents per hour.

Football was not the only sport Lou played at the college. He participated in lacrosse during the spring seasons of 1959 and 1960. His brother Paul played on the team as well. Paul arrived at UNH in 1958 and the brothers were reunited again. His was the first freshman class at the school to receive full sports scholarships and Paul was a recipient. During the 1960 season, UNH had a home match against Tufts University. Lou injured his knee and was sidelined. While Lou was out of action a Tufts player came after Paul with a lacrosse stick. Lou went after the Tufts player and the Tufts team jumped on Lou. Then Lou Sr. came out of the stands and within moments, it was the D'Allesandro family versus Tufts. The trio acquitted themselves quite well, as the rest of Wildcats contingent looked on. "We were the talk of campus," Lou laughs as he recalls the melee. "If they thought we were a little crazy that may have resolved all doubts."

There were lots of transformative moments during Lou's college years. There were opportunities for growth and new experiences. In the spring of 1960, D'Allesandro was exposed to an event that would trigger an interest destined to become a great part of his adult life. Senator John F. Kennedy was scheduled to make a campaign stop at the UNH campus. Lou felt a certain allegiance to the Democratic candidate for president. After all, as a congressman, JFK represented the 11th District, which included Lou's childhood East Boston neighborhood.[9] Unfortunately, Lou got to the event late. An overflow crowd caused officials to close the building to additional attendees. D'Allesandro was disappointed but undaunted. He cased the building for another entry point and settled on a side window. "I pried the window open and hoisted myself up and through it," remembers Lou with a big grin. "I fell further than I anticipated, I didn't realize it, but I was over a staircase and I tumbled onto the stairs. A guy reached out a hand to help me up." "Hi, I'm John Kennedy," quipped the charismatic candidate. Lou reacted quickly, "Hi, I'm Lou D'Allesandro." It was an indelible moment, the type of exchange one never forgets. "Meeting him was unbelievable – he was a presence and a very good speaker," recalls Lou.

The day changed a lot for Lou. "It really juiced my interest in politics," Lou reflects. He never imagined then the role he would someday play in Democratic presidential politics. In the short term, Lou set out to prepare himself for a potential foray into politics. "I signed up for a class titled 'Discussions and Debate.' It was an English Department offering and the instructor was Marge Williamson," Lou notes. The course was a good choice. Williamson was the sort of instructor who was fully invested in her students, especially those who had strong motivations. "She really wanted to help," Lou says.

Politics would also help shape Lou's last college summer. On July 6, 1960, President Eisenhower, fuming over the nationalization of U.S. property in revolutionary Cuba, effectively cut off U.S. imports of Cuban sugar.[10] Lou got himself a job as a stevedore at the Domino Sugar facility in Boston. He would help unload the holds of the last freighters of sugarcane imported from Cuba that summer. Domino paid Lou $2.62 per hour. It was the most money he had ever made. The work was hard; the men loaded 100-pound burlap bags of sugarcane onto conveyors to be boiled into refined sugar. Lou remembers how well everyone got along, black union workers and white college kids. "It was a great group of guys and we were fully integrated." Not only was the Cuban sugarcane running out that summer, but the old plant was being scrapped for a fully automated one. "It was the last hurrah."

Before heading back to school, Lou used his earnings to buy a 1959 Rambler. He adorned it with a vanity license plate, "Del 1." It cost an extra $25 for the special plate. "One of the black guys thought I was a VIP," laughs Lou. At the end of August, Lou packed the Rambler with his belongings and "Del 1" made its way to Durham and D'Allesandro's last college football camp.

Lou was a co-captain of the team for his senior season. The other captain was Paul Bellavance. The team opened its season with a one-point loss, 7-6. Dartmouth, the team's rival for fifty-nine years, stopped the Wildcats' comeback bid on a failed extra point at the one-yard line. The Wildcats were convincing at home, winning every game played on the Durham campus. Those home field wins included impressive outings against conference foes Delaware and Connecticut. It was the first time the Wildcats had beaten the Blue Hens, and the Wildcats handed Connecticut its first Yankee Conference loss in six years. Unfortunately, the Yankee Conference championship was decided by a loss to the University of Massachusetts in the last game of the season.

Lou and his fellow co-captain were invited to the New England Sports Writers Dinner in Boston. They were accompanied by Chief Boston and received some recognition for the season's efforts. For its efforts, the football team was feted at a field house banquet after the season ended. Frank Leahy, who played on one Knute Rockne's fabled "Fighting Irish" Notre Dame football teams, was the featured speaker. By 1961, Leahy was already a coaching legend himself. When he appeared at the Wildcat banquet, the All-American and future NFL Hall of Fame inductee had just served as the general manager during the inaugural season of the AFL's San Diego Chargers. What Leahy told the young gridders that night is probably lost to time, but it's a pretty good guess that one of his most famous quotes might have served as some sound advice that night. "When the going gets tough, the tough get going."[11]

Lou's days in Durham were coming to an end. He had much work ahead of him, and an entire future to secure. When the fall semester concluded, Lou left the campus with only six credit hours left to complete for his degree. His dad and stepmother were going to Florida and needed someone to be at the home in Medford to keep an eye on Lou's youngest brother, Henry. This was very difficult for Lou as it meant that he would not be able to play lacrosse or take part in all the activities at the end of his final semester. He would not be able to leave UNH on a high note, but there was no reasoning with his dad. Lou finished his coursework at Boston University during the spring semester, juggling his time working for his dad's business and taking care of Henry.

Once graduation came, Lou was forced to put his Marine Corps plans aside. Surgery to repair a knee injury prevented him from becoming a "regular." Instead, D'Allesandro was placed in a reserve unit. College graduation would mean an entirely new set of plans.

CHAPTER 5

The Start of Marriage and Career

Lou's college graduation was followed by the best decision he ever made. He married Patricia "Pat" Morganstern on May 27, 1961. The nuptials followed a two-and-one-half year engagement. Lou had popped the question at a frat party during the fall of 1959, the couple's sophomore year. The ring he selected for the big night was a beautiful antique setting that had been his mother's, fitted with a new diamond. When the time came, Lou had an economy of words. "I just handed it to her and said, 'here.' I was so romantic," he laughs. Fortunately, Patricia knew it was coming, so the brevity of the exchange didn't bother her or require a whole lot of explanation.

It didn't take long before the new bride would be tested by the "in sickness and health" part of their vows. Two weeks after the wedding, Lou underwent surgery at Massachusetts General Hospital to repair the knee injury that foiled his military career. The operation was more complex than first thought. The problem started with a football injury that was later exacerbated by some "friendly fire" on the lacrosse field. His brother Paul accidentally rolled into Lou's knee when the two collided while crisscrossing the field. Word about the lacrosse injury got around the campus quickly. Says Lou, "I walked into class, and the professor pointed out the incident, titling it the story of 'Cain and Abel.'"

When the surgeon went to work, he found that a portion of Lou's knee cartilage had broken off and it was jammed into the knee joint. The doctor had to cut the medial collateral ligament to remove the cartilage and only then begin the process of repairing the knee. Lou explains the rudimentary nature of physical rehabilitation in those days. "We didn't have good rehab, I was out of school and with no training facilities I had to do the rehab on my own."

As Lou worked himself back into shape, the newlyweds spent their first summer in three different homes. They lived with Lou's father and then with Pat's parents. Their third stop was a small apartment in Manchester near Pat's parents' house that the new couple sublet. By August Lou had his first job. The position satisfied his affinity for the New England landscape. Kennett High School, located in Conway, New Hampshire, collected about five hundred students that attended Grades 9 through 12 from its host town and five other surrounding ones.[1] Nestled in central New Hampshire's White Mountains, and on the Maine border, Conway had a population of just fewer than 4,300 in 1961.[2] Everything was located on Main Street. The school, the town's one movie theater (which was open only on weekends), the laundry, and Hills IGA grocery store, were all located near the D'Allesandros' fifty-five-dollar-a-month apartment behind Chet Ballou's Shoe Store.

Kennett paid Lou an annual salary of $4,400. In return, he taught US, world and European history, civics and business math. Outside the classroom he served as the school's head football coach and assistant basketball coach. Lou didn't have much time to prepare for football season. The challenge was intensified by the sheer distance some of the players had to travel to school. Some of the students boarded their school bus at 5:00 AM. If they played football, they would be on the last bus out at 6:00 PM. By the time some of the players got home, they had put in a grueling fourteen-hour day. Lou's commute was far more abbreviated. His apartment was so close to the school that Pat could look out the window and see the football field. With a bird's-eye view of the practice, she knew precisely when to get dinner. If Lou thought he was going to have a supportive staff on the football field, he was misguided. He had two assistant coaches, but according to Lou, "one knew almost nothing about football and the other one was a skier."

The Kennett School Eagles did not fly as high as the surrounding mountain tops in their debut game under their new head coach. The team lost to Lebanon High School 7 - 6. As far as Lou was concerned, the team just didn't play hard. "It still hurts," he says with a smile. "I started 'firing' players who weren't performing," he recalls with a humorous glint in his eye. "Then the team captain approached me, 'Coach we don't have enough players.' I had to call some of the players back off waivers." As the season progressed, the new coach settled in and the team learned his expectations. Lou swapped the team's black jerseys for white ones he foraged from Chief Boston at UNH. Local radio broadcaster Bill Clapp interviewed Lou before football games. Clapp's daughter Nancy was one of Lou's students in history class and Clapp's wife worked with Pat at the Carroll Reed Ski Shop in North Conway. Clapp's son Gordon went on to an acting career with credits that include a starring role in the television show *NYPD Blue*.[3] It was a close-knit community as only a rural New Hampshire town can be and the D'Allesandros made a lot of good friends there.

One of their great friends was Karl Seidenstuecker, who happened to be the previous football coach at the school. "Karl was a great mentor to me," notes Lou. Besides teaching at the school, Seidenstuecker owned rental cabins and a restaurant. Lou pitched in at the restaurant by washing dishes when help was needed. Those were simpler times. The D'Allesandros remember how monumental it was to purchase their own washing machine. Once installed in their apartment, they proudly showed it off to every guest who visited. Today they get a good laugh out of how understated things were in the sleepy little town.

If the high school football season had a highlight, it was the Thanksgiving game with traditional rival Berlin High School. Kennett entered the game with a 3 - 4 - 1 record. "The team got more enthusiastic as the season progressed," its first-year coach recalls. "We beat Berlin handily and ended the season even." Lou took the boys to UNH to see a Wildcat football game with tickets generously provided by Coach Boston.

Lou's reception in Conway was positive but it soon became clear to him that life was a little too slow there. "We were too far from civilization, so we moved," D'Allesandro says in forthright terms. Their destination, East Boston, couldn't have been more different from the tiny town of Conway. Lou went back to work for his father and Pat got a job at the phone company. She didn't like her new surroundings. "There wasn't a blade of grass and I didn't know anyone. I would have gone anywhere else," Pat notes candidly. As it turned out, a potential job opened for Lou in Pat's hometown. She could not have been more pleased by the prospect of going home to Manchester.

Bishop Bradley High School needed a head football coach and there wasn't much time to hire one. The all-male Catholic school thought they had their candidate, but the prospective coach withdrew from the position in mid-summer. Lou secured an interview and Brother Adrian, the principal, offered him the coaching position and a few more duties as well. The job included teaching American history, civics and biology. "I was one chapter ahead of the students in biology class," Lou chuckles. Then there were the sporting duties. He was assigned to the head coaching role for the football and baseball teams and named an assistant basketball coach. For the entire gamut he was paid $5,000 annually, with no health insurance and no pension. Brother Adrian did hold out the incentive of a bonus if Lou could draw a large enough attendance at the football games.

Pat transferred her phone company job to New Hampshire and the couple found themselves renting another Manchester apartment. It certainly felt like home, at least to Pat. After six months living on Hanover Street, they returned to the apartment they sublet the previous summer at 16 Tilton Street.

In the fall of 1962, Lou took up his duties at the Manchester private school. He would spend a busy four years there. His football acumen was part of the reason he ended up at Bishop Bradley and the season reached full crescendo just as it should – on the final game played Thanksgiving Day. Bishop Bradley faced the Manchester Memorial Crusaders at Gill Stadium. The Catholic boys led the Crusaders in the game, 8 – 6. At one point, the Crusaders were forced to punt. The Bishop Bradley player got close enough to the kick for the referee to rule that it had touched him. and Manchester Memorial recovered the ball deep in Bishop Bradley territory. That was only the beginning of the controversy. Lou didn't see the play the same way the referee did, and he let him know about it in strong terms. "It was lousy," recalls Lou. Those types of plays never turn out well and this one was no different. The Crusaders capitalized and scored the winning touchdown. Lou wasn't finished. Even then he had all the "no-quit" in him that would serve him well in politics.

"I went crazy over the call," D'Allesandro says without qualification. "I vowed to never use officials from the New Hampshire Interscholastic

Association ever again. I tried to replace them" Lou's plan was thwarted by the school – Brother Adrian was more diplomatic. "I was forced to write a letter of apology," says Lou. It wasn't just a private note to the officials, but a letter to the newspaper for all to see. While Lou remembers the play and its aftermath with precise detail, he can't recall if Brother Adrian ever paid him the bonus for filling the seats. "It was an up-and-down season," notes Lou. "I came in late and changed the system all around."

Coaching high school football was not the only way Lou got the game out of his system. He donned a uniform and played on a number of semi-pro football teams in the 1960s. Back in those days, semi-pro players got paid. Lou started with the Providence Steam Rollers for $25 per game and then went on to the Boston Nu-Way Sweepers for the same pay. His third and final stop on the semi-pro circuit was with the Lowell Giants, a farm team for the Green Bay Packers, where he played linebacker for $135 per game.[4] The Giants cycled a lot of talent through their ranks into the pros. One of the Giants' alums was Tommy Dempsey, a field goal kicker who held the NFL field goal record for forty-three years with a 63-yard boot on November 8, 1970 at Tulane Stadium.[5] The historic kick earned the New Orleans Saints a 19 – 17 win over the Detroit Lions as time expired.[6] There were others. At one time or other, Lou played alongside Bob Tucker, who became an all-pro end with the Giants; Dick Capp, who went on to play linebacker for the Green Bay Packers; and future Oakland Raider players with such unforgettable monikers as Jim "Jetstream" Smith and "Moonshot" White.[7]

On September 16, 1966, Lou played his last football game. Quitting wasn't a voluntary thing; he was enjoying football as much as he ever had. That night the Giants hosted the Scranton Miners. Co-captain D'Allesandro intercepted a pass from his linebacker position and ran it back for a touchdown. It was a great night – that is, until a crack-back block reinjured the knee that kept him out of the Marines. The team's doctor was also on the Boston Bruins' staff. He sent Lou on an ambulance ride, and it was back to Massachusetts General Hospital, this time for a total knee reconstruction. Lou asked Pat if she saw his big play earlier in the night. When she nodded approvingly, he thought at least he went out in a blaze of glory and his wife witnessed it too. It wasn't until later that she admitted to never seeing the play. She decided he needed all the support he could get when he was in the hospital. It was his last football game as a player.

In a twist of fate, the couple's first daughter was born that very day, although they didn't know it at the time. Pat had trouble conceiving and two months later, they adopted their first child, Anne-Marie. The D'Allesandros welcomed their baby into a home they had purchased on Harriman Street the year before. In the autumn of 1966, Lou moved on to both fatherhood and a new job. His latest position was at the New Hampshire College of Accounting and Commerce, most often reduced to the acronym "CAC" (pronounced "cack").

It wasn't his first involvement at the school. As early as Lou's second year at Bishop Bradley, he worked part-time at CAC. The fledgling business college, which conferred its first associate's degrees that year, hired him to institute and coach a basketball program. He also worked part-time as CAC's athletic director. The Bishop Bradley program had been quite successful, and it put Lou on the map. By contrast, the college program needed some work. CAC was a two-year school on the second floor of a downtown Manchester office building. There was no campus or gym when Lou worked there on a part-time basis.[8] Basketball space had to be rented elsewhere. Despite the austerity of the facilities, Lou got the program off to a good start.

When he committed to the college full-time in the fall of 1966, Lou served as the athletic director and a history professor in addition to continuing his duties as the basketball coach. (There was no football program). Budgets were still tight; Pat laundered the basketball uniforms. But if the team's resources were limited, its fortunes on the court were not. "We were very lucky," Lou remembers. "We never had a losing season." In his ten years at the school, Lou saw a lot of changes along with even more wins on the basketball court. While Lou compiled a winning percentage of .745 (117-40), the college earned the right to confer four-year degrees in 1966 and shortened its name to New Hampshire College three years later.[9] In 1971, the college moved from downtown Manchester to a 300-acre campus on the Merrimack River. Today the school is known as Southern New Hampshire University.[10]

The D'Allesandro family saw some changes of its own in 1968 when they welcomed their second child, Michael, in November of that year.

Before they celebrated their seventh anniversary, the couple and their two children were well settled in the Manchester community. It was time to seize the future and look ahead to new challenges. In retrospect, Lou's next step was fairly predictable. He entered politics.

Like many Americans, Lou was transfixed by the television coverage of the Kennedy assassination in 1963. He couldn't help but remember meeting the charismatic JFK just a little more than three years before when JFK was campaigning at UNH. It left a deep impression on him and an interest bubbling under the surface. In the summer of 1964, Lou and Pat visited Washington and the grave of the 35th president. In those days it was surrounded by a white picket fence that formed a 20-foot by 30-foot plot. The permanent memorial was still three years in the future when Lou gazed upon Kennedy's final resting spot.[11] It was a moment that gave rise to some deeper thoughts. His college years had provided plenty of opportunities to take charge. Lou was well-liked. His colleagues on the football field and classmates on campus respected him and expected him to lead. Those who knew him best may not have been surprised when he threw his hat into the ring for a position on the Manchester School Board during the fall of 1968.

As Lou characterizes that first run for public office, "I put my name in against a guy who had been in forever." His first foray in politics was as a Republican. "I was following my father's lead in the choice of party." Lou Sr., who was previously a Democrat, was persuaded out of the concept by Massachusetts Governor and Democrat Paul Dever. Dever was elected the Commonwealth's governor in 1948. In 1952, after an unsuccessful bid for the Democratic presidential nomination, Dever came under fire for increasing the pensions of former state legislators. One of those was the infamous James Michael Curley, who was not only a former mayor of Boston and governor of the Bay State, but also a convicted felon.[12] The elder D'Allesandro found very little appealing in Dever. Compounding the realities of Massachusetts politics was the gulf between Italians and the Irish. It was all too much for a heating contractor from East Boston to take – he switched his party and became Republican. Lou ran for the Ward Ten seat. That ward is still part of the district he represents today. The core of the ward, then and now, is solidly Democratic. The outcome was fairly predictable. It didn't end well. The entrenched incumbent, in Lou's words, "trounced me." Despite the disheartening result, Lou was hardly dissuaded from trying again. To the contrary, the experience merely emboldened him to master something he was admittedly a neophyte at. His political journey had only just begun. There were many more races and battles ahead.

CHAPTER 6

Politics and Basketball

Lou made another attempt at elective office in November 1970. It was his first run for state representative and the outcome of the race was a much closer contest than in his first election. The votes for the state representative's race were cast at a district firehouse. When the polls closed, the paper ballots were collected and carried upstairs to be counted in a smoke-filled room. Once again, Lou lost to a Democratic incumbent. Despite what ended up as a very narrow loss, Lou didn't request a recount.

Today, Lou reflects on his first two tries at public office. "Timing is everything in life, I had too many other things going on in my life at the time." Lou was truly a busy man. Beyond his full-time teaching duties at New Hampshire College, he was raising a young family and coaching basketball as well. In fact, Lou's involvement in basketball had expanded since arriving at the college.

It was a pure quirk that led Lou down a new basketball path in 1967. In those days the glare of highly polished television productions and mega-contracts for players were still years off for the NBA. Franchise owners employed a variety of tactics to fill stadium seats. Double-headers and exhibition games were all part of the fare. So were preliminary games played by college teams at the Boston Garden. CAC and other members of the Greater Boston Small College Conference appeared in those contests. During one of those Boston Garden games, Satch Sanders, a member of the Celtics' roster and a future Hall of Famer, asked Lou if he could warm up with the college kids.

It was all a bit surreal. "Our kids were going through the layup line," recalls a smiling Lou, "and there is a starting forward for the Boston Celtics in uniform going through the line with us taking his layups." That night sparked a lifelong friendship between Sanders and D'Allesandro. It was also the beginning of a boys' basketball camp that the two men started the same year. Satch and Lou were joined by Don Nelson, another Celtics player, and the three partners opened their camp. They chose Camp Litchhaven, a very rural setting, in Litchfield, New Hampshire, as their venue. The work involved recruiting campers and other professional basketball players to help run a week of instruction and fun for the kids. "In those days, we could bring in pros for reasonable fees," notes Lou. Within a few years, the camp went co-ed and expanded to two weeks. When the camp grew, the partners moved their operation to New Hampshire College to hold their third season.

The camp attracted a group of colorful basketball aficionados who pitched in to make things work. There was a furniture store owner from New Hampshire who helped out with recruiting. He happened to be a good friend of Johnny Most, the legendary voice of the Boston Celtics. The furniture executive ended up compiling statistics for Most to use during his iconic broadcasts. "It was a fun time," Lou remembers. "It put me in contact with a lot of pros. I got to travel with the Celtics to a few away games." Lou remembers one particularly amusing anecdote when he ended up joining the team for a game at New York's Madison Square Garden. "I went into the Knicks' locker room and one of the players said, 'Hi doc,' [because] they thought I was the team physician. All of a sudden, in walked Bill Bradley wearing a blue Princeton blazer, a pair of khakis and saddle shoes – looking very much in Ivy League style. Eventually, they figured out I wasn't there to attend to their team's medical needs and I got ushered right out of there."

The basketball camp and contacts with professional players were not the only unexpected benefits from college coaching that Lou experienced in his early career. In 1970, Lou coached his New Hampshire College basketball team in a game against a traveling team from Great Britain. The local team beat the British contingent handily. In the wake of the international tilt, Lou was approached by the Brits to become a technical adviser to their Olympic basketball team. At that point teams were already preparing for the 1972 games. During the summer of 1970, Lou found himself taking a series of trips to the United Kingdom to recruit and train the best British amateur players.

The British team's manager was Bernard Warden. Lou lived with Warden on the outskirts of Bracknell when he wasn't traveling throughout the United Kingdom. Warden had an older brick home without central heat. "It was a cold flat," Lou remembers. Warden's home was a contrast to the center of Bracknell, an area built after World War II that featured a pedestrian-only town center.[1] On one of his United Kingdom trips, Lou gave lectures on basketball coaching in Scotland, first at the University of Edinburgh and then at Saint Andrews. The talks were a part of a Federation of International Basketball (FIBA) conference. In Scotland, Lou's international basketball contacts expanded even further.

It was there on the Scottish Southern shore that he met Janos Szabo, a Hungarian who had only become a basketball coach after retiring from a world-class soccer career.[2] During World War II, Szabo fought in the resistance and when the Communists took over the country, he was jailed. Even in 1970, his return trip to Hungary was secured by a family-held hostage back at home. In addition to Szabo, Lou met basketball officials from such far-flung places as Greece and Yugoslavia. Soon after, coaching offers followed from a number of different nations seeking to establish improved basketball programs, but pragmatism dictated that Lou keep his job at New Hampshire College. Lou's basketball acumen was certainly getting wide notice.

D'Allesandro traced his coaching talents to a variety of sources. Coach Seidenstuecker from Kenneth High School preached the fundamentals of the game. There, Lou was exposed to an offensive philosophy that emphasized a crisp and deliberate passing. Every player touched the ball as the team worked for the best shot. Lou's second mentor was Coach Frankie O'Donnell at Bishop Bradley. O'Donnell's teams notched 55 wins and two state championships while Lou was on O'Donnell's staff. The philosophy at Bishop Bradley was different than at Kennett. O'Donnell ran the fast break. The center was counted on to take down defensive rebounds and make a quick outlet pass down the court. The offense at Bishop Bradley was wide open. It had a certain free-form quality to it that encouraged greater creativity from the players.

The element that couldn't be taught was something Lou had possessed before ever stepping onto the court as a coach. A good coach must be able to teach. His players need to be receptive to the lessons that will be the foundation of their success. "I was fortunate to have great rapport with my players," Lou observes. During his own school years, Lou had exercised a great deal of leadership among his peers and football teammates. Translating that leadership to coaching was a natural extension of something started during his years on the gridiron. Lou had long been a keen competitor and that suited his coaching style and career well.

He took that belief in winning with him to Great Britain in the summer of 1971. Only two weeks before Lou made his overseas coaching trip, Pat gave birth to the couple's third child, daughter Christina. Despite their new addition to the family, Lou would be working with the British team for six straight weeks. It was time to form the nucleus of the British Olympic Team. The summer included tournament play in Europe, as well as a tour of the U.S. and Canada. After a slate of games, the team went to Augsburg, Germany, to play in the Olympic qualifying tournament.

"We weren't very good," Lou admits. "We won a few games, it was a great learning experience." The British team didn't qualify to compete in the Olympics.[3] Lou thought the spirit of competition was wanting, especially with the British coaches. "It was a play-to-play attitude, not a play-to-win notion," Lou recalls. "They even call the games 'friendlies.'" There was a gulf in thinking between the British coaches and myself." Lou felt that they just weren't working the players hard enough. He tried his best to instill a sense of pride and urgency. "I wrote to the Queen and asked to have her meet the players at Buckingham Palace." The Queen did not receive the team. Apparently, she had no time for anything as trivial as the national basketball team. But the squad did get an audience with another dignitary that summer. It would be hard to imagine meeting anyone more important.

The Pope sponsored Catholic games that summer and the British team competed. The teams marched into the Palazzo Dello Sport, a venue that hosted basketball competition during Rome's 1960 Olympic Games.[4] The Italian tour also included an invitation to the opera from the Pope. But the unquestioned highlight of the summer came when Lou and the British team had a private audience with the Pontiff at the papal summer residence, Castel Gandolfo. The team assembled in a small room and anxiously awaited Pope Paul VI. Suddenly, the smallish and frail supreme Pontiff entered the room. He was assisted by attendants as he walked to his seat. Lou remembers the event with the same awe as the day it happened. "We were only feet away from the Pope and outside there were crowds screaming 'Papa-Papa!' It was a great moment, something you never forget."

When the basketball trip ended, Lou returned to New Hampshire, his young family, and a new semester at the college. Lou learned, with great astonishment, that his international basketball travel was not quite finished. Bob Raiche, an administrator at New Hampshire College, was instrumental in developing a cultural exchange between New Hampshire and the City of Fortaleza, Brazil. In 1963, then-President Kennedy inspired the launch of the Partners of the Americas program to encourage a people-to-people exchange as part of his Alliance for Progress – an economic cooperation between the U.S. and Latin America.[5] Eight years later, the State Department awarded its first educational and cultural grants to promote exchanges between the partners.[6] The New Hampshire partnership was one of the first under the program. Fortunately or unfortunately, Lou was dispatched to Brazil to conduct basketball coaching clinics in furtherance of the brand-new exchange.

Before all of the foreign policy and Kennedy administration programs could sink in, Lou's plane landed at an airport serving the Brazilian State of Ceará. Lou got a crash course in South American security. Immediately upon landing, the plane was surrounded by machine gun-toting troops, some boarded the plane, a number climbed onto the wings, and still others examined the luggage. The military presence was overwhelming. There was a guerrilla insurgency at the time and terrorism was a reality in South America's largest nation.[7] Lou remembers, "They told us not to answer the phone or the door at the hotel unless we were absolutely certain of who was calling."

If there was anything that made the basketball ambassador feel a bit more comfortable, it might have been the ethnicity of the region. A large percentage of the population, including the state's governor, was of Italian descent. "We were treated royally," Lou recalls. He was a guest at the governor's palace and was transported to the official residence in a government limousine. But even a simple limo ride brought home the danger that was always present. "I noticed that the doors of the limo were not finished with trim but remained hollow so they could be filled with machine guns," the touring coach recollects. "It was a police state."

The actual coaching in Brazil was somewhat impeded by the language barrier. Lou needed an interpreter to make his points. In addition to the need for translation, the facilities weren't very good. Lou had to get used to another feature of the culture. "We started each day on Brazilian time, which was always late. I got used to it after a while." Despite the hurdles, Lou enjoyed the coaching. "The kids were great and they loved to talk about California. Going there was their dream." The trip accomplished many goals of the exchange. Lou took away lessons from South America's largest nation. "The Brazilian people were a proud group, a warm and friendly people who loved my Italian heritage." Their interest in basketball was a harbinger of the country's leap onto the world basketball stage.

One of the highlights of the trip may have had little to do with basketball but instead another game. Lou discovered that the soccer great Edson Arantes do Nascimento, better known as Pelé was staying in his hotel. One of the greatest athletes the world has ever known was in town for a game. A crowd gathered outside the hotel and chanted the legend's name. Lou had the opportunity to watch Pelé play before returning to the U.S. from his two-week trip.

Once back in the states, Lou had his own match in 1972 – his third attempt at elected office. Against the backdrop of Lou's own campaign, the Nixon administration made diplomatic overtures toward the Soviet Union and China. Nixon redeemed a part of his pledge to end the fighting in Vietnam with honor by removing the final contingent of U.S. ground troops in August.[8] Earlier that summer, a little-noticed break-in at the Watergate offices of the Democratic National Committee was discovered by the Capital Police.[9] In August, the Democrats nominated Senator George McGovern for President and in November, Richard Nixon prevailed in every state but Massachusetts.[10] The Republican's landslide re-election was a good omen for candidate Lou D'Allesandro.

Lou's 1972 campaign for state representative took on a new level of urgency. "I worked at it," says Lou, "I knocked on doors and let people know I was very serious. At that time, there were a number of state reps who didn't do much." Despite Lou's increased level of effort, the campaign was low-key. There was no catchy slogan or media blitz, just a lot hard work. It was largely a one-man operation. Lou observes, "We had three young children at the time and Pat was very busy with the kids," so even home-grown assistance was very limited.

The bright October skies, decorated by splashes of fall colors, yielded to fallen leaves and gray skies. The voters of the 34th New Hampshire District went to the polls that November. When it was over, Lou had his very first election victory. "It was like winning a big game," notes Lou. "I went into it as an underdog and came out with a big victory." Nevertheless, there was no victory party or glorious speechifying, just a quiet recognition of achieving something new and important. He didn't know it then, but Lou had combined a number of qualities and knitted them into what would become a part of the fabric of his life. Many more elections lay ahead, inextricably bound to a lifetime of public policy initiatives and constituent service. In November of 1972, things were just getting started. But on that winning evening, not all thoughts were directed to the future. It felt good to achieve what the candidate remembers as, "a super victory and my first real adventure into winning politics."

CHAPTER 7

Building an Agenda and a College

In January of 1973, Lou D'Allesandro took his seat in the New Hampshire House chamber. It was a seat that clearly represented his status as a freshman legislator. "They put you as far away from the podium as possible and in the middle of a row," Lou laughs. The New Hampshire House is made up of four hundred representatives.[1] It has always been a citizen legislature, comprised of people from all walks of life. With a constitutionally mandated pay of $200 per term, it is little wonder that one-third of the legislature turns over in each biennial election.[2] Lou learned the ropes quickly and came to realize that there was one overarching truth that shaped how legislative business gets done in the Granite State. He sums it up in this way: "In reality there are about forty people who run the show – and sometimes, that's an overstatement."

Even a casual student of legislative machinations knows the importance of committee assignments. Lou's first term as a state representative included not only a favorable committee assignment but a focused fight over a highly substantive piece of legislation. The stage was set, in large part, by relationships Lou had forged at New Hampshire College. Kimon Zachos was legal counsel for the college, as well as Deputy House Speaker. "He was an influential and smart guy who had been a White House Fellow," Lou remembers. The White House Fellowship program was established by President Johnson in 1965 to provide highly gifted and motivated interns a year of service to senior White House and Cabinet secretaries.[3] Zachos' position in the House gave him great sway and he helped Lou get an assignment to the Education Committee.

The second twist of fate occurred when the topic of school lunches for the underprivileged ended up front and center before the Education Committee. Lou signed onto the School Feeding and Nutrition Act as a sponsor.[4] The issue that prompted the proposed legislation arose over a disparate treatment in the distribution of school lunches in the town of Claremont. An adjunct professor who taught law at New Hampshire College was working up a discrimination case to address the Claremont problem. The existing policy attracted attention when it was applied to brothers who attended different schools in the Claremont District. Each school had a different lunch policy. One brother was given lunch, the other was not. The legislation was intended to establish a uniform state policy on offering lunches in every school. A food stamp bill was introduced shortly thereafter.[5] "Both caused a furor," notes Lou.

There was a rough-hewn conservatism that prevailed in the Granite State and that was just fine with Republican Governor Meldrim Thomson. Thomson, who moved his law book company from the south to Orford, New Hampshire, had established his conservative roots in his native Georgia.[6] There were many Granite Staters who "didn't want anyone telling them whether their kids got fed lunch or not," according to Lou. Proponents of the law had a battle on their hands and Lou and his colleagues went to work.

"It was my first real grassroots campaign to pass legislation," Lou warmly recalls. "We went school to school, district to district." Lou had a great ally in the cause. The New Hampshire School Food Workers' Association labored along with the bill's sponsors. "The food workers were on the front lines. They were the people who looked into the faces of the kids who went without for lack of funds to purchase lunch. To them, the issue was particularly real," notes Lou. Nancy Stiles, the head of the association, capably led the food workers in the fight. She later became a colleague of Lou's in the New Hampshire State Senate.[7]

Approval in the House and Senate was not the only hurdle to the legislation's passage. Governor Thomson had to be convinced, and it was not a forgone conclusion that the legislature could override the Governor's veto. The School Feeding and Nutrition Act would provide Lou with an opportunity to lobby Governor Thomson directly. It was the beginning of a relationship with many twists and turns – most of which could be best described as dead-man's curves. Lou got an appointment to visit the governor at his office and the two men, both Republicans, discussed the bills. The meeting ended with nothing being decided. It was the first time Lou had a substantive discussion about anything with the governor. The fact that D'Allesandro and Thomson were both Republicans was about where the similarities stopped. Their first meeting would not be indicative of the nature of their future relationship. The initial consultation was outside the usual practice Thomson employed to meet legislators. Thomson had a custom of inviting legislators, ten at a time, to a pancake breakfast prepared by his wife Gail at the Bridges House, the New Hampshire governor's residence. What Lou will share about that practice is that "Gail was a wonderful lady."

In spring 1973, Lou's food concern was the act he worked so diligently to secure. The bill passed the legislature without an appropriation.[8] Lou is confident that if the bill had been accompanied by a spending component, it would not have become law. What saved the forward-thinking legislative initiative was a federal statute, The National School Lunch Act. The original federal statute was signed into law by President Harry Truman in 1946. The intention was to absorb American farm surpluses and distribute free or low-cost food to the country's school-age children. The New Hampshire Department of Education was allowed to tap federal funds, not only for lunch subsides, but also to equip the state's school cafeterias and promote nutrition education. Schools across the state were able to modernize their cafeterias while establishing a new curriculum intended to educate students about the benefits of healthy eating.[9]

The fight for school lunches did not end with the passage of the law. There were efforts to repeal the legislation during ensuing election cycles led by the state's most devout conservatives. Al Rock, a staunchly conservative state representative, was a "force to be reckoned with," according to Lou. The fact that Rock owned a radio station and newspaper in Nashua didn't dampen his appeal. Rock helped lead the repeal effort while Lou (still a Republican) had his conservative roots called into question. He was one of the few Republicans who supported the school lunch law. Ultimately, Manchester's *Union Leader*, a conservative newspaper and a strong voice in New Hampshire and beyond, dubbed

D'Allesandro, "Liberal Lou." The *Union Leader's* publisher was the irascible William Loeb, who announced his moniker for Lou in a name-calling front-page editorial that labeled Presidents Eisenhower and Ford as "Dopey Ike" and "Jerry the Jerk." It was pretty impressive company for a legislator from New Hampshire, in spite of the pejorative labels.

The *Union Leader* benefited greatly from New Hampshire's first-in-the-union presidential primary. The electoral idiosyncrasy and Loeb's unflinching brand of conservatism made the newspaper one of the best-known small-city publications in the nation. Ironically, Lou's political role and stature would ultimately benefit from the same presidential primary preeminence that the *Union Leader* did. But as to political ideology, Loeb and his newspaper couldn't be more different from Lou, who sums it up like this: "As a Republican, I was too liberal, and as a Democrat, I was too conservative. Political life was always going to be hard – things would never be easy."

In 1974, significant political opportunities as well as challenges loomed. Lou ran for two political offices that year. One was far more difficult than the other. In the spring he was elected a delegate to New Hampshire's Constitutional Convention. It was the sixteenth convened in the Granite State since 1775. The purpose of the convention was to consider revisions and amendments to the state's constitution. Since the 1974 convention, the voters of the state have only authorized one additional convention, the seventeenth in 1984.[10]

Quite apart from constitutional theory, the real challenge in 1974 was presented by a vacancy on the Executive Council. New Hampshire elects five Executive Councilors from respective districts divided according to population. The Council has authority to approve or disapprove of the governor's nominations, in accordance with Article 47 of the state constitution. John Bridges, a Republican, was the incumbent councilor for the district in which Lou resided. The New Hampshire governor's residence bore his family name in honor of ancestors who donated it to the state.[11] Bridges' run for Congress in 1974 created a vacancy on the council. A departing incumbent usually creates an intense competition for an open seat and that was the case for the District Four Executive Council seat in 1974.

The Republican primary for District Four featured a tough three-way race. Lou was the decided underdog. His opponents included Bob Rivard, a gas station owner and popular Golden Glove fighter, as well as Roland Tessier, an insurance executive. It was a very contentious race that at one point degenerated into a fistfight between rival partisans during a standoff on Elm Street in Manchester. Despite his underdog status, Lou had an edge that his adversaries did not fully appreciate. He had the benefit of a very loyal base of supporters who had been his students and athletes. "They carried me through," Lou exclaims. In the process, he pulled off a huge primary upset. In what was a clear contrast to the more staid reaction after his first political victory two years previously, a big party at the D'Allesandro home followed the stunning victory. Lou prevailed in the general election, beating the Democratic nominee Ed Cassidy, a Manchester alderman.[12]

It was the start of a new chapter for Lou. "This race set the stage for my political life," he thoughtfully reflects. "It was a big turning point in my life. It elevated me to a place where I was becoming a player." The win created another reality. He was also on a collision course with Meldrim Thomson. D'Allesandro's clashes with Governor Thomson were as predictable as getting jolted on an amusement park bumper car ride. The ultraconservative curmudgeon ran for governor in the 1968 and 1970 Republican primaries. Thomson lost the nomination on each try, but in 1970 he ran in the general election on the third-party ticket of the American Independent Party. It was the same far-right organization that nominated Alabama Governor George Wallace in his 1968 presidential election bid against Richard Nixon and Hubert Humphrey.[13]

Thomson finally succeeded in 1972 when he ran for governor on his pledge to veto any new taxes and prevent any increases to existing taxes. His rallying cry was, "Ax the tax."[14] Thomson's fanatical conservatism wasn't limited to fiscal matters. During Lou's first term on the Executive Council, one of Thomson's feature moves included threatening to cut all funding to the University of New Hampshire after a gay student organization held a dance and performed a play on the campus.[15] The following year he proposed to arm the country's National Guard units with tactical nuclear weapons at a meeting of the National Governors Association.[16] What Lou described as a "time of turmoil" was just beginning.

Lou's new political duties were not the only changes afoot. His political rise had gained the attention of Warren Rudman, the New Hampshire Attorney General. Rudman was on the board of the New England Aeronautical Institute (NEAI), a two-year college in Nashua.[17] The school was in trouble. The board received a report recommending the two hundred-student institution's closure. Amid the financial chaos, Rudman approached Lou and asked him to become the college's executive vice president. The move would be risky. Lou negotiated a departure with his superiors at New Hampshire College, but they agreed to allow him to return to his position at the college if the move to the new school didn't work out. With that assurance in hand, D'Allesandro readied himself to take on the Herculean task of righting a sinking ship.

When Lou arrived in Nashua, the NEAI board removed the incumbent president but inexplicably kept him on the payroll for a short time. Ultimately, Lou became the college's president. Lou quickly realized that the job would entail a top-to-bottom restructuring. The school's mission, aviation and air traffic control training, had to be expanded. A broader curriculum was accompanied by a new brand and a forward-thinking marketing plan. The school's name was changed to Daniel Webster College.[18] Lou went to the legislature to obtain authority to grant four-year degrees, and he earned a measure of credibility for the renamed school by obtaining membership in the New Hampshire College University Council. Every day required an exhaustive cash flow analysis – a daily recapitulation to determine whether, at least on a short-term basis, the bills could get paid. Lou had the assistance of one of his former students from New Hampshire College who was an accounting major. At one point, a bit of relief came in the form of a $150,000 loan Lou secured from a local bank. He learned the very important lesson of signing it in a representative capacity as the college's president. There was clearly some risk in whether the loan would ever be fully repaid.

In addition to financial distress, there were other, more tangible signs of mismanagement at the college. The dorms were falling apart, and the school had a half-finished gymnasium. Lou had to take action to show students and prospective students that the college had a new vitality. The dorms were so bad that the resident students were in a semi-revolt. Lou went to work. He went to the U.S. Department of Housing and Urban Development (HUD) and got help to rehabilitate the units and catch up on long-deferred maintenance. In addressing the unfinished gym, Lou took a more "hands-on" approach.

Lou rolled up his sleeves and went to work. He helped dig the trench to connect the gym to the public sewer line. He painted the walls and shoveled snow off the roof. His commitment became more evident with each shovel of earth or paint brush stroke. Lou called in favors from tradesmen to complete the necessary subcontract work. He ruffled some of the trustees' feathers when he sold one of the school's prize assets, a Ryan S.T. training plane, to the Owls Head Transportation Museum in Maine for $25,000. The funds were a welcome shot in the arm in the effort to get the gym finished. Opening the gym was a huge step in establishing the viability of the college going forward. It demonstrated to the students that the conditions at the school were improving. "It was something the students needed to see," according to Lou.

Lou's hard work at the college paid dividends in multiple ways. Warren Rudman, who initially tapped D'Allesandro for the role, not only watched his charge succeed with the difficult task, but also got himself elected to the U.S. Senate in 1980. A positive relationship with Rudman wouldn't hurt Lou's own political future, nor would the credit that came along with his success as the rescued college's president.

To say Lou was busy in 1976 would be a grand understatement. The new college job required a longer commute and his work on the Executive Council kept him occupied as well. On top of that, his Council seat came up for re-election during that same hectic year. Lou would be the first to admit that none of it would have been possible without his wife. "Pat was a rock," Lou acknowledges. "She kept the house in order and allowed me the freedom to pursue all of those roles." With all the challenges of a young family, it is remarkable what the couple was able to accomplish. Despite his success in education and politics, there were still many hurdles ahead, and more goals to be achieved. The place Lou occupied on New Hampshire's political stage was about to be further tested. Meldrim Thomson, the colorful governor, was clearly in Lou's path.

CHAPTER 8

A Councilor Takes on the Governor

America celebrated its bicentennial in 1976 and Lou's political experience, especially with Governor Thomson, may have resembled some of the rancor of the nation's revolutionary times. It was an election year for Lou, but long before voters in the Fourth District went to the polls, the councilor had his hands full with Governor Thomson and his conservative cheerleader, William Loeb. The *Union Leader's* publisher showed a great penchant for supporting the far-to-the-right Thomson.

An appointment by the governor to the Health and Welfare Commission formed the backdrop of one of the year's critical standoffs between Thomson and Councilor D'Allesandro. Lou smelled a "good ole boy" relationship among Thomson, his appointee, and Loeb. He questioned the administrative capacity of Thomson's choice, thinking the decision was dictated by patronage and not the interests of New Hampshire's citizenry. Lou couldn't support Thomson's pick and Loeb went to work to discredit the Fourth District Councilor because of it. In an editorial appearing in the *Union Leader* on May 7, 1976, Loeb wrote:

> *The newspaper is frankly puzzled as to what's gotten into Councilor D'Allesandro. Over the years, this newspaper has had a very pleasant relationship with the Councilor and has publicized his successful activities as an athlete and as a coach.*

It was as if Loeb thought D'Allesandro owed him something for the prior favorable press coverage associated with his achievements in the sports world. The factious newspaperman feigned a complete lack of knowledge relative to Lou's failure to support Thomson's pick for Health and Welfare. Instead of debating the merits, Loeb went to work, and further underscored his ire over Lou's failure to approve of Thomson's selection. The *Union Leader* publisher was anything but complimentary:

> *AGAIN, IT SEEMS TO THIS NEWPAPER THERE MUST BE SOME HIDDEN SPECIAL INTEREST OR SOME HIDDEN GROUP OF INDIVIDUALS THAT HAS COUNCILOR D'ALLESANDRO ON A STRING AND IS MANIPULATING HIM LIKE A PUPPET.*

> *We cannot imagine that the Lou D'Allesandro of old with whom we had so many pleasant relations at the newspaper, could be acting in this strange fashion of his own free will.*

> *Certainly, if this continues, we think that many of the voters who supported D'Allesandro last time will change their minds and get behind someone else for the Fourth District.*

The governor's first choice for Health and Welfare was not confirmed, despite the protestations of Loeb.[1]

Loeb wasn't done with D'Allesandro, but before Lou turned his attention to the fall election, he had other work to do. While his re-election effort was sure to be opposed by New Hampshire's largest and most vocal newspaper, Lou put aside his full attention to politics for other pursuits.

Once again international basketball called. This time it was an Eastern Bloc country. Athletics generally, and basketball in particular, were of growing importance in the Soviet Union and its satellite nations. Janos Szabo, Lou's friend from his basketball trip to Great Britain, convinced Hungarian authorities to secure Lou's services as a basketball consultant. Szabo enjoyed great popularity among his countrymen from his days as a soccer star. The Hungarian national team was preparing to participate in an important Eastern European tournament and Szabo was able to use his credibility to convince authorities to secure the services of D'Allesandro for the tournament.

As a result of Szabo's recommendation, Lou got a call from the U.S. State Department notifying him of the overseas assignment. Looking back, Lou observes, "Athletics has always been a convenient way to promote good relations between nations." He was supplied with a diplomatic passport and off he went to Hungary during the summer of 1976. When he arrived in Budapest, he was greeted by a Russian army officer who would shadow him throughout his two-and-one-half-week trip. His entire visit to Hungary was surveilled by the communist authorities. Home during his stay was a Soviet military base. Despite the ever-present eye of Moscow, Lou managed to enjoy the trip.

He had an opportunity to swim in Lake Balaton, the largest freshwater lake in Central Europe. The long, finger-shaped lake has long held an important place in Hungarian history. Balaton was a resort for the Hungary's aristocracy but by the late nineteenth century the railroads brought the country's middle class to its shores.[2] Near the lake, Lou visited a three-hundred-year-old Catholic church. As a stark reminder of heavy-handed Soviet rule, Szabo was forbidden to enter the church even though it had been closed since the Communist Party came to power.

When Lou wasn't sightseeing, he was training the Hungarian team. He remembers, "The talent was good. The players were very attentive and did everything by the numbers." While in Lou's estimation the Hungarian players had a good understanding of the game's fundamentals, they had a few shortcomings, too. "What they lacked was the improvisations of the American system and native talent," recalls Lou. Despite those differences, Lou saw a significant difference in the way the game was played in Hungary as opposed to the United Kingdom. "It was a big contrast from the Brits; the Hungarian players wanted to win badly."

For his trouble, Lou was paid a thousand dollars a day in Hungarian currency. There was little practical value to payment. He bought a few things to bring back home and gave the balance of the Hungarian currency to Szabo. When the trip came to an end Szabo got very emotional. The two men realized it was likely to be the last time they would spend any time together. As the two men said their goodbyes, Lou reflected on Szabo's trip to the United States in 1973. Lou took his

Hungarian friend to an NCAA Basketball championship game in St. Louis where they witnessed the UCLA Bruins defeat Memphis. Today, Lou recalls his friend's fascination with some familiar aspects of the American landscape. Szabo was transfixed by McDonalds, supermarkets and the other everyday fixtures of American neighborhoods. Before Lou left Hungary, he gave Szabo his Converse sneakers, the balance of the basketball equipment he brought with him, and a ring from the University of New Hampshire. As Lou boarded a Hungarian Airlines jet to London, Szabo was moved to tears. "He was an emotional guy." Lou remembers., "It was the last time I saw him."

After a layover in London, Lou made his way back home. During the summer of 1976, the country was in a celebratory mood. Across the nation, Americans were commemorating the two-hundredth anniversary of the country's independence. Stanley Hamel, chairman of the New Hampshire House's Transportation Committee, was appointed to New Hampshire's American Revolution Bicentennial Commission by Governor Walter Peterson in 1969. Hamel spent thirteen years as the commission's treasurer.[3] Representative Hamel had Lou appointed to the Bicentennial Commission and with that, the Executive Councilor developed a full slate of duties connected to New Hampshire's bicentennial ceremonies. Lou's new responsibilities included a national bicentennial meeting in Saratoga Springs, New York, and participation in an endless succession of parades throughout the cities and towns of the Granite State. Parades meant the participation of Pat and children, with countless smiles and waves as the family visited one town after the next. "It all got to be a bit too much," Lou remembers. "The children were pleading, 'Mommy, do we have to go?'" He understood their plight.

If that weren't enough, there was the Councilors' airplane tour. Fellow Executive Councilor, Ray Burton, nicknamed "Burton for certain," would charter an aircraft for an excursion to visit the state's airports. This was a natural extension of Burton's North Country philosophy and he "obliged" his fellow councilors with a sort of barnstorming tour of New Hampshire's air transportation capacity.

When Lou was finally able to put his travels abroad and in-state behind him, he got down to the business of campaigning. True to his May threats, Loeb went on the offensive. In spite of his conservative pedigree, second to none in the Granite State save perhaps the right-wing, jingoistic Thomson, Loeb backed a Democrat against Lou in the general election. Loeb's selection in the Fourth District Executive Council race was Lucille Kelley. Lou's challenger was one-half of the Manchester advertising agency of Cohen and Kelley. Apparently drawing on her professional expertise, Kelley coined a promotional slogan for her campaign with an unmistakable patriotic flair. "Born on the Fourth of July" was her mantra long before the Tom Cruise movie titled with the same phrase. One can only imagine the glee that Thomson and Loeb, flag-waving wordsmiths that they were, felt for Kelley's most appropriate birthday.

Lou's 1976 election was emblematic of a number of difficulties brewing in New Hampshire politics. Lou was still three election cycles off from changing his party affiliation. Still a Republican in 1976, he had a front-row seat to the turmoil brewing in the party. Governor Thomson was creating a schism in the New Hampshire GOP. Lou represented the moderate wing of the party and the governor anything but that. In Lou's estimation, Thomson's aim was to create a shadow form of government, one where he surrounded himself with like-minded cronies so all control was centric and his. That wouldn't do for D'Allesandro, and the more Thomson dug in his heels, the more Lou opposed his maneuvers.

A resounding victory by Lou over Kelley in the November election did nothing to quell the bitter divide. The first months of Lou's new term on the Executive Council were dominated by a spat between the majority of the Executive Council and the Governor over the re-appointment of the New Hampshire State Hospital superintendent to a new four-year term. Lou and three of the other four councilors favored re-appointment of the incumbent superintendent, while Thomson had other ideas.[4] Lou and other councilors consulted with the Health and Welfare Advisory Board, a key player in the appointment process, and the Governor, assisted by Loeb, criticized the councilors in the press for holding secret, clandestine meetings. One of Thomson's supporters minced no words:

> *While I cannot evaluate all of the members of the council, I can state unequivocally, that Mr. D'Allesandro is not qualified in any way to provide direction to the Governor in the operation of the state.*[5]

For his part, Lou made it clear that the meetings were no secret and the governor had been invited to attend. He noted that the members of the Advisory Board were quite informative and helpful, especially in the case of the other three councilors who were new to the job. In actuality, the appointment of the state hospital superintendent in New Hampshire was supposed to be made by the State Director of Mental Health in consultation with the Health and Welfare Advisory Board, but Thomson wasn't about to let that thwart his goal to form state government in his own image.[6]

Council meetings degenerated into verbal exchanges and by March, Loeb picked up his acerbic editorial pen and went on the attack again. This time he took on not just Councilor D'Allesandro but the whole notion of an Executive Council altogether. In an editorial titled "A Dog in the Manger," he wrote:

> *Four members of the Governor's Council, Raymond S. Burton of Bath, Malcolm McLane of Concord, Mrs. Dudley W. Dudley of Durham and Louis D'Allesandro of Manchester may not realize it, but they are doing the state a great service by venting what this newspaper can only describe as a VICIOUS attitude toward the governor and meeting secretly to discuss ways in which they can thwart the governor.*
>
> *They are illustrating the fact that the Governor's Council is a hangover from another age and is a stumbling block on the road to good government.*
>
> *These councilors are a perfect example of WHY the Governor's Council should be abolished.[7]*

Loeb's March invective wasn't finished. On the 29th he penned an editorial titled, "Three Kooks Kick the Shoeworkers." The head man at the *Union Leader* started his remarks, as usual, with feigned astonishment.

> *It is perfectly incredible that the Governor's Council would vote to table Governor Thomson's resolution in support of more protection for the U.S. shoe industry. It is particularly amazing that Councilor Louis D'Allesandro,*

who comes from Manchester, where many people work in shoe factories, would lead this action.

Thousands and thousands of shoe workers in New Hampshire and all across the country have already lost their jobs because of foreign competition from shoe producers in countries where the wages are only a fraction of those paid in the United States.[8]

Lou will tell you that Thomson's gesture was an empty one, the sort of political machination high on showmanship and woefully short on substance. President Carter wasn't going to take policy cues from the right-wing governor of New Hampshire and anyone in tune knew how empty the governor's gesture truly was.

No description of Thomson would be complete, however, without recalling his reaction to the Clamshell Alliance. The Alliance was a group of protesters opposed to the construction of the nuclear power plant at Seabrook. In late April 1977, 2400 protesters descended on the site to stage a civil rights-style encampment. A village was set up, complete with tents, portable toilets and self-imposed curfews and other rules.[9] If the protesters thought their numbers imposing, Thomson was not intimidated. The next day, he assembled a task force of state troopers augmented by their counterparts from Vermont, Connecticut, Maine, and Rhode Island. The coup de grace was Thomson flying to the site by helicopter, dressed in military fatigues and ready to direct the arrest of some 1414 protesters.[10] It was the sort of spectacle that the governor relished.

If the governor enjoyed his public persona, the voters of New Hampshire were not having the same experience. In the fall of 1978, Thomson lost a re-election bid to Democrat Hugh Gallen.[11] If anyone thought that Thomson was finished with politics, they would have been mistaken. Lou's re-election to the Executive Council the same year yielded a term without Thomson. While matters in the short term would be different, that didn't mean Lou was done with the surly archconservative. Their paths would cross again and help define Lou's political future for years to come.

CHAPTER 9

Primary Battle

I n 1980, Lou made a rather fateful decision to seek the Republican nomination for governor. His opponent, and adversary, Meldrim Thomson, furnished a large portion of the motivation for his campaign. Lou simply refused to join Thomson's "good old boy" network, and the butting of heads that started during Lou's first days on the Executive Council showed no sign of abating. In reality, Lou was up against far more than Thompson himself.

There was no dispute that Thomson had a firm hold on the conservative base of New Hampshire's Republican Party. Lou had carved out more moderate positions that, among other things, distinguished him markedly from Thomson. But when Lou ran against Thomson he also took on William Loeb, Thomson's unequivocal political ally. Loeb's *Union Leader* was New Hampshire's only statewide newspaper and to make matters worse, it was published in Manchester, Lou's home base. By the time Lou entered the fray for governor, Loeb was already practiced at disparaging D'Allesandro. He had already dubbed him "Liberal Lou," a label that wasn't fair, but that didn't matter to Thomson and Loeb as they skillfully made sure the false label stuck.

Taxes were of the greatest importance to New Hampshire's Republican voters and there was not any substantive difference between the candidates on the issue. Both Thomson and D'Allesandro opposed the creation of state income and sales taxes. Yet early in his political career, Thomson made claim to tax opposition ascendancy with his well-ingrained slogan, "Ax the Tax." Thomson, with the help of Loeb, was successful in claiming the role of the anti-tax savior to the exclusion of D'Allesandro.

According to Lou, "Pat was a hundred percent against my running for governor." Her reasons were very straightforward. She had an intuitive sense that the public wasn't ready for it – an Italian-American as governor of the Granite State. Pat also knew that the campaign would have financial ramifications. The process would require Lou to leave a good job as well as make a commitment of personal resources to the election effort. To make matters worse, Pat shunned the limelight. Being the First Lady of New Hampshire wasn't anything she was interested in or would enjoy.

While he may have had a different opinion at the time, Lou would now agree with his wife's wisdom, that running in 1980 was the wrong thing. "As I reflect back, it was probably the stupidest thing I've ever done," admits D'Allesandro. "I thought it was the right time, but I was totally incorrect." Lou was riding a wave at the time. He had spent successful years on the Executive Council and his work to save Daniel Webster College had earned him a great measure of credit in New Hampshire circles. But as Lou now reflects, "It is hard to gauge the intensity of the wave." Without the benefit of hindsight, Lou entered the fray with a belief that he could win.

Lou attempted to draw Thomson into a debate, but the brusque conservative wasn't taking the bait. In temperament and ideology, there were clear differences between D'Allesandro and Thomson. The former governor correctly assessed that there was no advantage to him in having those differences underscored. Lou challenged Thomson and his Republican loyalty. In mid-August, Lou charged;

> *The real question is, where is Meldrim Thomson, and*
> *what is he doing, and what party does he belong to now?*
> *If he wants to be the Republican nominee, Mel Thomson*
> *has got to defend his record.[1]*

Lou made it clear that Thomson had abandoned the GOP in 1970 to become a member of the American Party, the same political organization that facilitated Alabama Governor George Wallace's run for President in 1968.[2] In 1979, the ex-governor ran a short campaign for president as the representative of the Constitution Party, a political faction he created in his own image. Lou pressured Thomson for an explanation;

> *The public deserves to know where Mel Thomson has
> been the last two years, what happened to the Constitution
> Party and why he left the Republicans.*[3]

D'Allesandro wasn't getting any answers or a debate, and neither was the public.

A week after Lou called out Thomson on his party affiliation; the *Concord Monitor* published a story on the campaign resources of the candidates for governor. At that point, Lou had raised more than double the amount that Thomson had, $81,650 to $37,098. By contrast, the eventual Democratic nominee and incumbent governor, Hugh Gallen, had raised $193,442 by the same point. Lou's financial lead would be short-lived as Thomson displayed the power of the conservative wing of the party.[4]

On Monday, August 26, 1980, the Thomson campaign hosted six hundred donors at a $100-per-plate chicken cordon bleu dinner at the Highway Hotel. The former governor reportedly raised $100,000 that night. In his dinner remarks, Thomson looked past D'Allesandro and attacked the re-election efforts of both President Carter as well as New Hampshire Governor Hugh Gallen. The *Concord Monitor* report noted highlights of Thompson's speech:

> *"I do not believe that this country can survive as a free
> nation with four more years of Carter as president," he
> told his audience. "Nor do I believe that our state can
> survive as a beacon of hope to the other states of our
> nation, and a bastion of fiscal sanity, with two more
> years of Gallen as governor."*
>
> *Thomson called Hugh J. Gallen a governor who "suckered
> the voters on a promise to reduce their light bills,"
> discouraged job opportunities, obstructed the construction
> of the Seabrook nuclear power plant, failed to protest the
> opening of "an abortion mill" in Portsmouth and turned
> a state budget surplus into a deficit.*
>
> *"Look at the horrible mess our people face," he said,
> "because a Gallen administration has tried to sail the ship*

*of state with rotten canvas imported from Massachusetts
political sailmakers and a rudder heavy with the barnacles
of bureaucracy."*[5]

The dinner's featured speaker could not make it. Utah Senator Orin Hatch sent a letter explaining he couldn't leave Washington because he was in the process of fighting a $65 million appropriation sought to provide federal assistance for victims of family violence.[6]

The dinner's rhetoric was not limited to an attack on liberal spending and related causes. A story appearing in the *Concord Monitor* the next day quoted a former Executive Councilor from Milford on D'Allesandro's chances in the nomination fight. Fred Fletcher, a supporter of Thomson's, didn't think D'Allesandro had a chance. The newspaper reporter wrote:

> *"A lot of people disapprove of some of the things Thomson
> did," he said, "but all in all, he was a hell of a good
> governor. And he's gotta have the money."*
>
> *Fletcher added that he wasn't really worried about Thom-
> son's chances in a primary against a Republican with an
> Italian surname.*
>
> *"Lou D'Allesandro's a nice guy," he said. "I have nothing
> against him. But you know, and I know, that a lot of
> people in this state vote the name."*[7]

Lou took umbrage with Fletcher's insinuation. While it was pointed out that the critical portion of the newspaper account was not a direct quote, Lou believed Fletcher's premise was abundantly clear. Fletcher himself ran unsuccessfully for governor in 1962. The former pol, who operated a chain of paint stores in New Hampshire, stayed away from the controversy.[8] However, that didn't stop Thomson from getting involved. Thomson decried Lou's complaint as a "desperate vilification of me and my campaign." For his part, D'Allesandro viewed the smear as business as usual from Thomson and his supporters. At a news conference held in the wake of the remark, D'Allesandro said, "This character assassination is standard procedure for Mel Thomson and his supporters. It is obvious to me that the Thomson campaign is using tactics common to the John Birch Society."[9] Even if that weren't so obvious, Thomson was an active member of the ultra-conservative, anti-communist organization.

In 1981, when the John Birch Society was planning a university in New Hampshire, the *Nashua Telegraph* published an editorial piece on the subject. The writer quipped parenthetically: ("Can you picture Meldrim Thomson, who has been an active member, as a university president.")[10]

In the face of the acerbic battle, Lou tried to turn the focus back to the improvement of government. After all, it was political factionalism and favoritism that created the gulf between D'Allesandro and Thomson in the first place. Lou focused his campaign on good government through effective management. He summarized his theory that good management meant "hands-on, working knowledge of government. You're meeting with department heads, you're reviewing budgets, and you're starting with budgets from a zero base. The budgeting process is key." At least one Associated Press writer noted that Lou's platform was not overly exciting. "It is not a subject to stir the souls of voters..." wrote Gary Langer in the *Concord Monitor* on August 29. Lou minced no words in the face of the ho-hum pan of his platform. "I'm not a damn political animal. I'm me, and I'm not going to change, I don't want to be a phony."

If there was an issue of the times, it might have been the Seabrook nuclear power plant, then under construction. It would have been hard to find a bigger supporter of Seabrook than Meldrim Thomson. D'Allesandro's position was different. Lou didn't believe the first reactor should be operated until the federal government devised an effective method to dispose of nuclear waste and developed a workable evacuation plan for the seacoast population. One of the hot-button fights regarding Seabrook was the planned second reactor. On that topic, Lou said this:

> *"I don't think (reactor) two is needed," he said. "We must develop alternative energy sources – low-head hydro, solar, wood, maybe tidal, maybe the importation of some excess hydro from Canada."* [11]

On March 28, 1979, Pennsylvania's Three Mile Island nuclear plant suffered a partial meltdown.[12] The experience of Three Mile Island certainly helped crystallize Lou's position regarding the second reactor at Seabrook. Plans for the second reactor were stalled in 1983 and scrapped in 1986.[13] According to the experts, Lou's campaign was as big a longshot as the doomed second reactor. While most thought Lou was facing very significant odds, there was some speculation that his background as a popular athlete, coach and college president might pay dividends. David Rinds, the executive director of the Republican state committee, noted, "He (D'Allesandro) has enormous contacts with kids who are now young adults, and he has sports connections. A lot of people know him and respect him for those endeavors and his work down at the college." [14]

On Tuesday, September 9, Meldrim Thomson prevailed in the Republican primary. In what was described as a low voter turnout, Thomson outpolled D'Allesandro 55,554 to 40,060. [15] Less than a week later the two men attended a Republican unity breakfast. Outside the event, and in front of reporters who were excluded from attending the breakfast, Thomson walked up to D'Allesandro and "thrust out his hand for a handshake." Lou shook Thomson's hand, but did not end up endorsing Thomson's candidacy. The endorsement was withheld despite an offer by the Republican candidate and his supporters to help retire Lou's campaign debt. Lou agreed to support the GOP ticket in November, but no more. [16] In the end, Lou had more in common with the Democratic nominee, Hugh Gallen, than he did with Thomson. Gallen won the general election and in the process vindicated at least some of D'Allesandro's platform. "I walked a thin line," remembers Lou. "I was in the wrong party. The Republican Party was splintering and the moderate wing of the GOP was disintegrating."

In the aftermath of the election, Lou's problems were far more tangible than the future of the GOP in the Granite State. He had a sizable campaign debt that he converted to a loan for repayment. Compounding the problem of campaign finances was the loss of his lucrative job as the president of Daniel Webster College, which he had quit to pursue the governor's office. Through all the rancor and obligations surrounding the campaign, Pat held the D'Allesandro household together. All the stresses and strains of child rearing were magnified. The kids were finding their own way and had their own needs. Then there was the matter of making a living.

For the first six months after the election, Lou worked at a mental health center in Derry. He was responsible for grant writing and community relations. In early 1981, the president of New England College called and asked Lou to help with problems at that school. He was appointed Executive Assistant to the President and began a daily fifty-minute commute to the one-thousand-student college in Henniker. His duties included maintaining a positive relationship with the college's bankers, who were looking to work their way out of underwriting the school. He was successful in maintaining a positive climate with the banks which involved monthly update meetings. He was also asked to supervise the maintenance of the college building and grounds, another talent he had honed at Daniel Webster College. His standing at New England College slipped when the president resigned. The new appointee and Lou didn't get along. Fortunately for both parties, a solution was at hand and Lou was loaned to the New Hampshire College and University Council to work on a student admissions project.

While Lou had employment, there was little doubt that anything with his professional or political life was yet settled. "It was a time to regroup," he recalls. There were many lessons from the election try. He learned a lot about people and the value of relationships. He learned how easy it was to misjudge the political climate and how politics could quickly create a false sense of empowerment. In addition to those essential truths there was another unavoidable observation.

A significant part of Lou's popularity derived from his former career as an athlete and coach. There were people who either resented or devalued what he had accomplished in education and politics because of his sports background. For good or bad, it was a reputation he had to live with in those days. Today, Lou estimates that twenty-two of his twenty-three colleagues in the senate don't know anything about his athletic career. But in 1980, that was a far different case. His stature as a former football star was so pervasive then that his son swore off the sport when his peers expected him to blossom into the same great football player that his dad was.

There were other concrete manifestations of the impact of sports on his career in those days. Lou recalls a meeting he attended with Mrs. Warren Rudman while president of Daniel Webster College. He and Shirley Rudman went to negotiate an agreement between the college and the Federal Aviation Administration relative to the school's air traffic controller training program. Shirley Rudman came away from the meeting impressed with Lou's ability, something she truly *wasn't expecting* from the former coach and football player. Even the meager praise

William Loeb offered Lou in the *Union Leader,* related to his athletics background, provided a hint. When criticizing Lou's politics, Loeb made it clear that, "the newspaper had supported D'Allesandro's athletic and coaching success" – carefully chosen words.

To be candid, however, it was not the root of Lou's popularity that derailed his campaign for governor in 1980. The ethnic issue was real in New Hampshire. Looking back, Lou notes, "I never realized that until the campaign was in full swing." It was a reality of the times, pure and simple. It was something Pat knew from the start. But to be fair, there were certainly other contributions to the end result. Lou didn't get the support from youth he thought might turn out. The populace wasn't as tired of Thomson as he calculated, and his own campaign lacked the experience and professionals that might have drawn a greater measure of support.

While there were lessons aplenty in defeat, Lou's discouragement was a short-lived thing. His commutes to Henniker were opportunities to do a lot of thinking. Almost from the beginning he rationalized that political success was often the product of repeated attempts. It did not take him long to begin considering his future and another run for office wasn't something he ruled out.

CHAPTER 10

Giving It Another Go

In New Hampshire, elections come and go as quickly as department stores rotate the stock of seasonal wares. It wasn't long after his 1980 primary loss that Lou set his sights on another try for the gubernatorial nomination of the Republican Party. The decision was firmed up in the late winter of 1981 and Lou began to assemble a staff. He was convinced that another try at the governor's office could make the difference. His prior run had earned him a greater state-wide recognition and he had a sense that this time the desired result could be achieved. It is often said that politics has a way of "getting in one's blood," and Lou was no exception. "Once you got a taste of it you get overcome with a sense that you can do it against the odds," Lou notes with a grin.

In addition to the foundation Lou had established with his prior run, there was another factor driving his decision to make a second attempt for the governor's office. The New Hampshire Republican Party was in a state of flux. The conservative wing of the party was gaining greater leverage and moderate views were being squeezed from the agenda. Lou thought that the 1982 election cycle might be the last time he could effectively promote a moderate platform as a Republican.

The 1982 Republican Party primary field featured no less than eight candidates, but Lou's principal competition came from two of them. One, John Sununu, was a 43-year-old mechanical engineering professor at Tufts University in Boston. Sununu, who held a doctorate from the Massachusetts Institute of Technology, was also a former dean at Tufts.[1] Politically, Sununu had served one term in the New Hampshire House of

Representatives, at the same time Lou did. His Republican credentials were strong enough to cause rumors that he was a possible choice by President Reagan for Energy Secretary.[2] The other principal competitor was Robert Monier, a 60-year-old retired geography professor who had served as an aide to former Governor Meldrim Thomson. Following his work for Thomson, Monier made a successful run for the New Hampshire State Senate in 1974. Five years later Monier forged a conservative coalition of Republican and Democratic senators to win the senate presidency.[3] There were clear differences between the contenders and Sununu did his very best to paint Lou as the liberal candidate.

For at least a decade, the front-and-center issue for gubernatorial candidates in the Granite State was taxes. Thomson gave the issue a brand with his "Ax the Tax" slogan and in 1982 candidates were being asked to take a "no new tax" pledge. Sununu and Monier took the pledge, D'Allesandro did not.[4] Budgets were tight in 1982 and the Republicans taking the tax pledge saw cuts as a viable solution to the state's fiscal problems. Lou's position was markedly different. The state couldn't afford more cuts. There were problems linked to shrinking agency budgets and those budget cuts still produced a deficit that was projected to go as high as $60 million dollars. With no state income or sales taxes in New Hampshire, there was a squeeze on property owners who shouldered the ever-increasing burden of real estate taxes. In an August interview in the *Concord Monitor*, Lou pointed out:

> *People are coming to realize that we have to have change because their property taxes have been impacted. They see the Laconia State School suit is lost. They see the prison problems. They see the state hospital problems. They don't like that. They do have a social conscience.[5]*

D'Allesandro's fiscal plan for New Hampshire was a lot more detailed than a simple "no tax" pledge. Officially referred to as "Revenue Reconstruction," Lou wanted a top-to-bottom examination of the state's revenue sources. It was a reform-style plan that was absent of any preconceived notions on which taxes should be created, adjusted, or eliminated. All potential revenue sources were on the table – income and sales taxes, a value-added tax or a land value tax. In addition to potential new sources of revenue, Lou wanted the legislature to look at a tightening of the business profits tax and an adjustment to the base of existing taxes such as the legacy tax. From Lou's perspective there was a revenue problem in the state and the responsible thing meant creating a fair sharing of the burden with the cooperation of the legislature. He made his position clear in an August 26th *Concord Monitor* interview:

> *D'Allesandro calls his plan for shoring up state finances "revenue reconstruction."*
>
> *That could mean any one of several new sources of revenue for the state – an income tax, a sales tax, a value added tax, a land value tax or a tightening of the business profits tax.*
>
> *D'Allesandro said he doesn't support any one of those plans more than another. Instead, he said simply that he will work with the Legislature on a plan for increasing state revenue.*
>
> *"I'm saying to them, 'We have a revenue problem,'" D'Allesandro said. "We'll talk about anything, but I want it to be fair and equitable.*
>
> *"I want to work with the Legislature. That's what I'm saying."* [6]

As unpopular as new taxes may be, especially through the looking glass of more than three decades, there were New Hampshire voters ready to support a revenue solution to their state's budget woes. Governor Hugh Gallen was proposing a plan similar to D'Allesandro's. Gallen beat Thomson, the ultimate anti-tax warrior, in the 1980 general election garnering, 59% of his vote tally from registered Republicans.[7] There was support for Lou's position within the party and he was confident that his honest approach to fiscal policy through effective management would ultimately pay dividends.

The fiscal condition of the state was not the only hot-button issue facing the candidates in 1982. The construction of the Seabrook Nuclear Power Plant was still creating a stir. More particularly, the question facing New Hampshire citizens in 1982 was whether or not to build a controversial second reactor. There was no doubt where Sununu came down on the second reactor. He was a strong supporter of nuclear energy, a position that nearly catapulted him to the nation's top energy job. Sununu believed that the completion of Seabrook was inevitable and that the Gallen administration was interfering with the efficient construction of both reactors by an over-regulation of the industry. He worried that Gallen's appointments to the Public Utilities Commission were hindering the construction of the nuclear plant. In late August, Sununu told the *Concord Monitor*:

> *"Seabrook is going to be finished," he said. "I think it is the responsibility of the Public Utilities Commission to protect the public interest. It is the responsibility of the management of that company to protect the stability of that company.*
>
> *"It is valid for them to be concerned (about the company's financial condition,)" Sununu said. "The responses they have made (the Public Utilities Commissioner) are not correct." [8]*

Monier was also an unequivocal supporter of nuclear energy, convinced that the completion of the plan would benefit New Hampshire taxpayers.[9]

Like the issue of taxes, the stances on Seabrook provided a clear distinction between D'Allesandro and his principal competitors for the Republican nomination. Lou didn't believe the second reactor was necessary or a benefit to the state's rate payers. As it turns out, D'Allesandro was proven right when the plan for a second reactor was later abandoned.

As significant as the differences were between the candidates, Lou and his competitors knew that the functioning of their campaigns and their ability to deliver support to the polls was just as important as the debate on policy. Lou tapped Peter Powell, son of a former New Hampshire governor, as his campaign chairman. Scott Kirby was installed as the campaign's manager and former Governor Walter Peterson and Stuart Lamprey, former speaker of the New Hampshire House of Representatives, advised and formed the campaign's inner circle. Statewide campaigns require outside consultants and the D'Allesandro organization utilized the services of the public relations firms for advertising needs.

The use of the radio and television media was a critically important part of the campaign effort and the D'Allesandro campaign turned to the Madison Avenue firm of Dresner, Morris & Tortorello. If you are wondering, the second name in the agency's title is Dick Morris, who would later come to fame as a political adviser to Bill Clinton and the White House when Clinton was elected in 1992.[10]

Today, Lou still maintains a carefully assembled binder that neatly contains all sixty-eight press releases issued by the campaign from June 1, 1982 through September 13, the day before the primary, in chronological order. The organization did a good job fundraising and was competitive, at least until the eve of the primary. The Republican candidates filed their finance reports with the New Hampshire Secretary of State's office on September 8, just six days before the primary. Sununu outraised all of his competitors with a reported total of $188,139. D'Allesandro was in second place, having collected $156,827. Monier was a distant third among the top-tier candidates with only $80,845 in fundraising.

Of particular interest was the $63,000 that the Sununu campaign amassed in the two weeks before the finance report was due. Twelve thousand dollars of the total came from a loan Sununu made to his own campaign. But another large sum in the amount of $20,000 came from four engineers who were employees at Marvin Engineering Company of Inglewood, California. Marvin is still in business and specializes in the design and sophisticated machining of parts for the aerospace and defense industry. According to Sununu, he met the four executives while working on Warren Rudman's U.S. Senate campaign in 1980.[11] After Rudman beat Sununu in the Republican primary that year, Sununu became Rudman's campaign chair for the general election in the successful senate campaign. In 1982, Sununu's press aide William Herman said, "Those were all people who supported Senator Rudman and they saw fit to support John." According to the *Concord Monitor*, Sununu also benefited from a $5,000 donation made by R. R. Barnacle, a self-employed sales representative in Cypress, California.[12]

In contrast to Sununu's report, D'Allesandro reported smaller individual contributions. The largest contribution, $2,009, came from his brother Paul and his sister-in-law Joyce. Walter Peterson gave the campaign $783 and Stuart Lamprey contributed $1,250. Two other donors gave $1,000 each: Gerald Zeiller, who ran unsuccessfully against Meldrim Thomson for the GOP nomination in 1976, and D.D. and Margaret Bean of Jaffrey, New Hampshire. Lou loaned his campaign $32,900, more than any other candidate.[13]

Lou's campaign was a true grassroots effort. The campaign was gathering steam and there was an unmistakable sense that a wave of support was growing as the primary neared. There was an auto tour from Colebrook to Seabrook with numerous stops in between. Lou remembers, "It was long and arduous." A former student of Lou's served as the driver. He worked so long and hard that the campaign gifted him the car when it was all over.

The campaign had great organizers and Lou recalls that Ann Powell, the campaign chair's wife, "ran as good a grassroots campaign as you could." Lou smiles as he remembers a grand spaghetti supper the campaign held. "My brothers Richard and Paul cooked the pasta," he says with a broad smile.

Despite the D'Allesandro ground game, Sununu was far from out of the running. The sizeable and late donated out-of-state money had a specific purpose. The Sununu campaign went to television and radio in a big way. It was a well-timed broadcast media barrage and there is little question that the advertising had an effect. The D'Allesandro campaign remained optimistic in spite of Massachusetts' Governor John Volpe backing out of a promised endorsement. Lou sensed a solid base of support going into the final days before the primary.

There was a sense of relief when primary day finally came. The results trickled in on election eve and Lou was ahead. The instant exit poll analysis of today was still years off in 1982 and hand-counted results had to be funneled to Concord before a winner could be announced. "I went to bed cautiously optimistic," Lou reflects. "I felt pretty good about the lead, but there were still ballots to count." When Lou arose in the morning he got ready to take the thirty-minute drive to Concord. His youngest child, Christina, went with him. They met in the campaign office with Scott Kirby, Walter Peterson and Stewart Lamprey. Kirby went over the numbers and delivered the unwelcome news. Sununu had won the nomination with 26,617 votes; D'Allesandro polled 24,163. Monier, who attracted the ultra-conservative Thomson Republicans, finished in-between with 24,823 votes. Lou walked over to the State House and formally accepted the result.[14]

The tally hit with a thud. "I had never been as low," says Lou. "To say I was devastated would be an understatement. It was like your life ended," Lou says with a dejection that still resonates all these years later. The euphoria and collegial feelings of the night before had vanished more quickly than the dollars flying out of the campaign coffers a week earlier. "I was thoroughly depressed," admits Lou.

"I had a feeling that I had let my supporters down." Thirty-five years later, he remembers the contributions of friends that gave their all to the effort. There was a successful pizza parlor operator Lou coached in high school who worked day and night despite the fact that a horrible accident left him as a paraplegic. There was a social worker who was a talented organizer and spent countless hours marshalling a solid base of support, and countless others who believed in Lou and his message. Suddenly, it was all over. If there was a tiny bright side, Pat escaped a limelight she never wanted.

In the wake of the primary, there were pragmatic concerns. Lou didn't care for Sununu and he wasn't about to endorse him despite both candidates having a connection to Senator Rudman. Sununu even offered to fundraise the retirement of Lou's campaign debt, but Lou still wasn't giving an endorsement.[15] In some ways, Lou's critics might not have been too far off when they criticized him for being too much like Gallen. Both men were moderates, and both rejected radically unflinching slogans calibrated to incite, not govern.

Gallen won the Democratic nomination and an opportunity to run for reelection. Lou didn't endorse the Democrat, but the two men met. Gallen promised to help Lou get a position in the administration at the University of New Hampshire. The plan was to name D'Allesandro as the public relations director for the college, a position he was well-suited to. Gallen never got a chance to make good on his offer. He lost the general election to Sununu and was quite ill at the time. He died before finishing his second term only a few weeks after the general election. Before his death, he yielded his office to Vesta M. Roy, the president of the New Hampshire Senate, who became acting governor for seven days until Sununu could be inaugurated.[16]

Lou was out of politics and out of work. Fortunately, Pat was working, but the D'Allesandros found themselves with a much-diminished lifestyle. Lou's campaign debt was retired by the sale of $100 tickets in a 50/50 raffle. He was out of work for the last six months of 1982 and once the primary was over in September, he was around the house a lot more. "It was pretty different," Lou observed. In January, Warren Rudman came through for Lou and got him a six-month position at a branch campus of UNH in Manchester.

If politics wasn't in the immediate future for Lou, there was a healthy measure of change coming. Transformative times were ahead, but that would not have surprised many who knew Lou D'Allesandro well. He had developed a knack for adapting to circumstances and the hard-fought battle for New Hampshire governor with its disappointing end presented a whole new set of hurdles for Lou to clear.

Lou with his basketball camp partners, left to right, Tom "Satch"
Sanders and Dave Cowens, NBA Hall of Famers and former Boston
Celtics, a visiting coach from France, Lou, Nellie Paquette and
Don Nelson, former Celtic, NBA Star and coach.

Lou coaching his New Hampshire College
team in the late 1960s.

Lou in his
University of
New Hampshire
football uniform
1960.

The D'Allesandro brothers, left to right,
Henry, Paul, Lou and Richard.

Lou announces a run
for New Hampshire
Governor in 1982.

Lou with former New Hampshire Governor Walter Peterson, New Hampshire College President Edward Shapiro and Senator Warren Rudman, Chairman of the Board of Trustees at Daniel Webster College.

Lou announces his switch from the Republican
to Democratic Party in June of 1985.

Lou and Pat sign their Democratic Party registration
forms at Manchester City Hall.

Lou makes a point during a press conference
announcing his new party affiliation as a Democrat.

On June 19, 1985, the Union Leader published this political cartoon noting Lou's move from the Republican to Democratic Party. House Speaker Tip O'Neil is at the helm of Lou's new party with less than good results in the opinion of the newspaper.

Cartoon courtesy of the *New Hampshire Union Leader*.

Lou announces his first try at elective office as a Democratic candidate for the Executive Council in June of 1986.

Pat and Lou at a postelection party held November 4, 1986.
Lou lost a close race for Executive Council that was
not decided until the following day.

Lou and Pat join Vice President Gore
at Manchester's Puritan Back Room in 2000.

Lou campaigns with Al Gore during the
2000 New Hampshire Democratic Primary in Manchester.

The *Union Leader* parodies Lou's attachment to expanded gambling revenue as a remedy to New Hampshire's education funding problems in 2005.

Cartoon courtesy of the *New Hampshire Union Leader*.

New Hampshire's largest newspaper reports Lou's 2005 support for expanded gambling as a solution to education funding needs.

Cartoon courtesy of the *New Hampshire Union Leader*.

Lou with President Clinton
at a White House Christmas party in 2007.

Lou campaigns with Hillary Clinton at St. George's Church
in Manchester, flanked by Chris Spirou, left
and Kostas Alexakis far right.

Hillary Clinton
and Lou appear
at a Manchester
coffee shop during
the 2008 campaign

Lou with President
Barack Obama and
Mike Lopez at
Sweeney Post Hall
in Manchester.

Lou debates gaming legislation in the Senate chamber.
Photo is courtesy of the *Concord Monitor*.

As Chairman of the Finance Committee, Lou holds the state's
operating budget as he makes a point during a senate hearing.

Photo is courtesy of the *Concord Monitor*.

Lou makes an emphatic point during a senate debate over the Birth Records Bill,
which proposed to allow adoptees to obtain their original birth certificates.

Lou tries an unusual form of transportation during a trip to Petra in Jordan during 2012.

Lou and Pat at a University of New Hampshire, Wildcats' football game in autumn of 2017.

Lou and Pat have shared a happy journey spanning six decades.

Lou and Pat with their family at Jenness Beach in Rye, New Hampshire.
Photo courtesy of Mallory Parkington.

CHAPTER 11

A Candidate Re-Invented

I n 1983, Lou was still in the midst of the tailspin that followed his gubernatorial primary loss the September before. "People didn't want to have much to do with you," Lou remembers. "People thought for all practical purposes that I was politically dead and buried." Lou learned that you just can't generate that type of energy and political hope and come to a crashing halt without consequences. His recovery would take time.

Fortunately, the life preserver that Warren Rudman threw him in the form of a six-month position with Merrimack Valley College got extended to a full year. The job was welcome, especially in the wounded state Lou found himself in. But the salary was half of what he had earned at Daniel Webster College three years before. There was little doubt that the position was a stopover, a place to adjust to some new realities and take stock of his future. Lou's tenure at Merrimack Valley would not extend beyond the one-year appointment. Life presented another opportunity and the resilient D'Allesandro, as always, answered the call.

When Lou was the president of Daniel Webster College, the school established a computer science major. Rich Lowney was one of the advisers who helped with the new program. By 1984, Lowney had launched a company called Computer Management Dynamics (CMD), which specialized in providing administrative software for colleges and universities. Lou knew little about the industry but decided to take Lowney up on an investment opportunity and a job. It cost Lou $40,000 for a five-percent stake in the company and he literally bet the house on the speculation. He raised the money by placing a second mortgage on his home and managed the new debt by making periodic interest payments only. Viewed in the most positive light, it was a gutsy move at best.

Lou went to work and learned the sales side of the business, including the management of the customer contracts. Selling and maintaining custom software proved challenging but the company experienced steady growth. Lou was a part of an important sale when the company secured a contract with a fledgling Phoenix University.

Eventually, Lou's association with CMD would pay off in multiple ways. One of the customers Lou called on was a small liberal arts college in Maine. Nasson College was founded in 1912 as a women's college at Springvale. The college went coed in 1952 and by the 1960s had grown into a well-regarded school with nearly one thousand students.[1] But by the time Lou visited the campus in the 1980s, things were in decline. The curriculum and physical plant needed a significant updating and the investor who had recently bought Nasson was looking for a new president to guide the process.

It was a job Lou was well-suited to and he readily admits, "Computer sales weren't really my thing." In a rather fortuitous convergence of events, CMD drew the attention of a group of foreign investors who were interested in meeting the growing company's capital needs. When the deal was consummated, Lou was able to sell his shares of CMD for $80,000, double his original investment, and take on the job of remaking Nasson College.

It would be hard to imagine a better outcome resulting from Lou's foray into the software development business than what he experienced at CMD. Nasson would provide an abundant challenge and round two in his college rebuilding career. As he looks back on his first days at the campus, Lou recollects, "It was in a state of disarray. The place had to be reconstructed. There was even a building that had been damaged by a lightning strike."

Not unlike his days at Daniel Webster, Lou called on friends and contacts as he planned to rehab Nasson. Those networks of people were instrumental in updating and creating programs at the college. He helped make the college more relevant. A sneaker manufacturer with a local plant had laid off a significant portion of its workforce. Those unemployed workers needed to be retrained with new skills to make them employable. D'Allesandro created a certificate program that provided those unemployed workers with computer skills. The liberal arts curriculum was updated and the physical plant rehabilitated. A mothballed science building was reopened and the library refreshed. Lou improved the relationship between the college and the Springvale community and is generally credited with making a positive impact at the college. His relationship with his employer is the story of another set of dynamics.

It is of some wonder that Lou was hired at Nasson in the first place. The investor that bought the ailing school, Ed Mattar, required Lou to take a psychological test as a condition of employment, something fairly uncommon for the times. According to Lou, "the test determined that Mattar and I were totally incompatible; he hired me anyway," D'Allesandro laughs. Lou remembers Mattar as being an "inventive guy" who created programs that credited life experience and other innovations that were precursors to online learning, but he couldn't take a word of advice. Officially, Mattar was the chairman of the Board of Trustees. "He conducted day-long meetings," recalls Lou. "He would set out a specific list of goals which one day even included a request that I fix his 100 mile-per-hour speeding ticket!" It was pretty clear that Mattar and D'Allesandro were heading in opposite directions and at a rate that was quickening as the months wore on.

The sweep of change was nothing new to D'Allesandro, but employment wasn't the only thing being reshaped in Lou's life. In 1985, Lou made a rather momentous decision that would have far-reaching consequences. In retrospect, it was something that began long before he reached a decision. While all the underpinnings were there, it still didn't diminish the profound nature of the choice. Lou and Pat headed to Manchester City Hall and, armed with a press release, they registered as Democrats. The chairman of their new party looked on. It was a bold decision with immediate ramifications.

The move brought an abrupt cessation to a number of friendships. This was predictable for a man with a political background as extensive as D'Allesandro's, but the expected nature of the backlash didn't make things any easier. In spite of this, Lou says, "I had no trepidations at all.

The Republican Party in New Hampshire was just too far-right. I was not going anywhere as a Republican." The loss of friendship was not the only gauntlet through which Lou would have to pass. There was plenty of criticism, especially from those who never liked him from the start.

It was no surprise that the *Union Leader* and its editorial staff would be chief among the detractors. Having long ago dubbed him "Liberal Lou," the conservative Manchester newspaper's editors unleashed a whole new wave of vitriol. In one political cartoon titled "In the Spring the Sap Rises," D'Allesandro is depicted standing on a downtrodden donkey. In a quote bubble, Lou states, "I have taken my dynamic leadership and inspiring ideas to a place where I'm appreciated." In the cartoon's final indignity, Lou wears a sandwich board sign that reads, "I am now a born for the – first time – Democrat. Liberal Lou." [2] On Friday, June 14, Jim Finnegan of the *Union Leader* published an editorial titled "Thank Goodness." The piece started with a hard jab:

> *It remained for Executive Councilor Bernard Streeter to sum up Republican reaction to "Liberal Lou" D'Allesandro's defection to the liberal wing of the state Democratic Party, whose principal achievement to date consists of the alienation of large numbers of the Democratic rank and file. Apprised of the move, Streeter said simply: "Thank goodness."*
>
> *A flippant remark? Not really. After all, there are other Republicans who, like self-serving "Liberal Lou," have turned their back on public sentiment on key issues while still remaining within the GOP fold. No, although we can't speak to Streeter's intent, we submit that far more than D'Allesandro's position on the issues, it is his attitude, his vindictiveness and lack of class, that have rendered him political persona non grata...*

In what appeared to be an effort to assuage the rancor, Finnegan concluded the editorial as follows:

> *Is it too much to hope that "Liberal Lou," who is a pleasant enough chap outside the political context, will clean up his act before he seeks elective office as a Democrat?*

Five days later, the *Union Leader* published another cartoon, this one featuring a sinking ocean liner named "Tip's (O'Neil) Titanic." While the ship is surrounded by the calamity of men jumping off it and swimming for their lives, a well-coiffed D'Allesandro in a gray business suit is climbing onto the deck as the large captain "Tip" says "Welcome aboard, Mr. D'Allesandro." Lou's defection from the Republican Party brought plenty of negative reaction; however, there was one interaction that transcends all of them for Lou. It is a memory seared into his heart and mind, the type of life lesson one never forgets, and it had everything to do with him becoming a Democrat.[3]

One of Lou's greatest political friends was Walter Peterson, a Peterborough Republican who served as New Hampshire's governor for two terms, 1969-1973.[4] Lou served in the House of Representatives during a part of Peterson's tenure and the men continued their relationship during Lou's time on the Executive Council. The two men "clicked," as evidenced by Peterson serving as the honorary co-chairman of the D'Allesandro's 1982 campaign. It was reasonable, especially given his experience with a number of other Republican friends, to wonder whether that would all change now that he was in the other party.

It had been nearly three years since D'Allesandro and Peterson had worked together actively in politics but when Lou revealed the news of his change in party to Walter, he was met with full acceptance. This didn't surprise Lou entirely, since he knew his friendship with the former governor was a solid one, but politics could test the strongest bonds. What Lou found remarkable about his post-Republican relationship with Walter Peterson was that the two men actually became even closer. In that experience, Lou may have learned one of the most valuable lessons of his political life.

Lou reflects on those years with great fondness. "He [Peterson] was an amazing man and his example to me was a positive lesson." Peterson was well aware of the political realities for Lou in the Republican Party. "He told me I wasn't going anywhere in the party and that my decision would never jeopardize our friendship." Peterson was a moderate and he knew that Lou shared that core belief. "He made it clear that basic values are distinct from politics," Lou notes. "The best guidance was simply to do what was right, not politically expedient." Unwittingly, Peterson was also teaching Lou how to "work the center." "It is important to be able to communicate with both sides," Lou observes. "The opposite poles of an issue are never good and won't produce compromise and progress."

Peterson's tutelage was not the only thing in their relationship that Lou benefited from. His mentor and friend also helped Lou out in a more tangible way. Peterson lost his re-election bid in the 1972 primary to fellow Republican Meldrim Thompson.[5] The incumbent governor refused to pledge a veto of any sales or income tax in the Granite State and "Ax the Tax" Thompson rode the fear of additional taxes to victory. Out of office, Peterson returned to private life and became the president of Franklin Pierce College in Rindge, New Hampshire. Peterson's own educational background included some well-regarded institutions. He attended the College of William and Mary, as well as two New Hampshire schools – the University of New Hampshire, and Dartmouth, from which he received a degree in 1947.[6] In 1988, Peterson hired D'Allesandro to oversee five branch campuses of Franklin Pierce that provided continuing education services. The division consisted of more than two thousand students and Lou held the job for nine years. His duties were wide-ranging and included budgeting and financial management, marketing, supervising all programs, faculty hiring and class scheduling. It was a job that called on the many skills and experience he had gained in education over the prior dozen years.

D'Allesandro's gratitude to Peterson is as strong today as it was the day he was hired. Lou readily admits that, "with his guidance, I made it through the storm cloud of politics – he made all the difference in my life." When Peterson died in June 2011, Lou gave his friend's eulogy. The tribute to his dear friend was heartfelt. "Next to my father, he was the greatest mentor I ever had." Governor John Lynch told the press something Peterson so generously shared with Lou D'Allesandro decades before. "Walter Peterson was always able to put partisan politics to one side and work with everyone just to solve problems and to make New Hampshire a better state.'[7]

In his later years, Peterson was well aware that his pupil had learned the lesson of "people over politics" well. It might have proved a great satisfaction to Peterson that Lou D'Allesandro took up the mantle of problem-solving politics. But before Lou could fully implement those lessons, there were years of elections and terms still ahead. Even before Lou went to work at Franklin Pierce, he had returned to the political fray with his first election effort as a newly minted Democrat. There was a long road ahead, with many hurdles, triumphs and travail, but this time Lou's philosophy was more in step with the party he was seeking to represent.

CHAPTER 12

New College, New Party

Lou's first foray into politics as a Democrat came in 1986 with another run for the Executive Council. The race had a number of dynamics that set it apart from his other campaigns, not limited to the obvious (Lou's new party). Lou took the job at Nasson after the decision to run and the continuation of his campaign had to be cleared with Ed Mattar. Mattar didn't object to Lou's campaign for public office, but he wasn't overjoyed about it either. The relationship between the two men was cooperative, at least in the beginning.

In time the relationship between the two would sour. To a degree, D'Allesandro and Mattar were working at cross-purposes. Lou had a vision for the school that included adapting the college to its surrounding community with an educational mission that served the school's market in an effective way. Mattar was more concerned with positioning the college in a way that maximized his profits. Mattar was a businessman and Lou was an educator. "He had a different game plan," notes Lou. "I had soon come to suspect he wasn't as concerned as I about how the college served its community."

"Mattar was a very different guy," remembers Lou. "He was hiring and firing people all the time. He threw lavish parties and loved to be liked." In spite of his business-first objectives, his educational innovations relative to life experience and online learning could not go unnoticed. Things didn't end well for Mattar. In November 2007, he took his own life, plunging twenty-seven floors from his Denver apartment window after breaking the glass with a sledgehammer. The day he died, Mattar was scheduled to be sentenced for his role in a multi-million-dollar bank fraud conviction in Federal Court. Lou wouldn't disagree with a quote from a story in the *Sanford* [Maine] *News*: "Mattar, who owned the former Nasson College in Springvale for a decade, left life much the way he lived it – with drama and bravado, and alone."[1]

To this day, Lou is mystified by the contradictions that were an integral part of Ed Mattar. When Lou finally left Nasson, Mattar shortchanged him $5,000 in salary. Years later, quite out of the blue, Mattar phoned his former president. "He asked me to forgive him," says Lou. "I was dumbfounded." The unpaid salary may not have been the only damage suffered by Lou as a result of his tenure at Nasson. His first race as a Democrat may have also been a casualty of his association with the college.

Lou won the Democratic primary for the Fourth District Executive Council handily, outpolling his closest rival, John J. McDonough, by nearly two-and-one-half to one, this despite taking a constant pounding from his old nemesis, the *Union Leader*.[2] In a June 3rd editorial, the newspaper took off the gloves:

> *The bad news is that Louis is leaving the Executive Council. The worse news is that Louis might replace him.*
>
> *Louis Georgopoulos, Executive Councilor for the greater Manchester area, gave up that seat in order to challenge U.S. Rep. Bob Smith. And that's been bad news all the way 'round.*
>
> *But even worse is that Louis D'Allesandro, in our book one of the poorest councilors in modern times, is trying to regain that seat.*
>
> *But there is good news, too. The good news is that Earl Rinker, Manchester's able Ward I alderman, has given up that safe seat and is likely to be the Republican nominee to face turncoat D'Allesandro come November's general election."*[3]

When Lou disagreed with Governor John Sununu's appointment to the New Hampshire Supreme Court as an overly partisan move, the conservative newspaper pounced again with equal vigor:

Turncoat-Opportunist

Only one who is completely bereft of a sense of humor would fail to get a chuckle out of the protest issued by "Liberal Lou" D'Allesandro, former Republican executive councilor now seeking a return to that post as a Democrat, against Governor Sununu's appointment of a conservative Republican, Superior Court Justice W. Stephen Thayer, to a vacancy on the state Supreme Court.

"Liberal Lou" is consistent, amusing [sic] so. As a Republican councilor he voted against qualified Republicans and as a Democratic candidate he's against...qualified Republicans.[4]

When the general election campaign got underway, the *Union Leader* seized on an issue that had little to do with D'Allesandro's ability to lead. Lou's appointment as president of Nasson in early October was the focus of the attack. Somehow the fact that Nasson's campus was a dozen or so miles from the New Hampshire border became of paramount importance. The *Union Leader* also took D'Allesandro to task on the fact that his appointment as Nasson's president was not immediately announced to the New Hampshire press, this in spite of the fact that the *Union Leader* routinely decided which of D'Allesandro's press releases it would publish. On October 21, the *Union Leader's* Jim Finnegan, not one of Lou's fans, wrote the following editorial:

Why?

Earl Rinker, Republican candidate for the Fourth District seat on the Executive Council, says he will "leave it to the constituents" as to whether "Liberal Lou" D'Allesandro's appointment to the presidency of little Nasson College in Springvale, Maine, has any bearing on his Democratic opponent's candidacy.

Well, this newspaper sees nothing wrong with it.

However, what may concern some voters is that appearance that D'Allesandro distrusted their judgment so much that he kept his appointment secret since he began his new duties back on October 2nd. Although the appointment was publicized in the Maine news media close to the college, no announcement of it was made to the New Hampshire press.

D'Allesandro's explanation that he isn't sure the appointment was of the "magnitude" to warrant letting Fourth Councilor District voters know about it is somewhat less than convincing coming from one who has never hitherto shown a reluctance to toot his own horn.

~ Jim Finnegan [5]

Today, Lou notes that Finnegan and his newspaper failed to mention at the time, that another Executive Councilor, Bernie Streeter, had worked at a hospital in Lowell, Massachusetts, for years – that simply didn't seem to matter. If Earl Rinker, Lou's Republican challenger, was initially ambivalent about the issue, his lack of concern faded in mere days. Rinker told the press that D'Allesandro's silence "was a deliberate attempt to deceive the voters of the Executive Council Fourth District. Lou D'Allesandro, who normally puts out a press release every time he sneezes, deliberately tried to hide the fact that he had taken a new job in Springvale, Maine, until after the election." [6] *The Union Leader* published yet another of its acerbic political cartoons. This one depicted Lou in his Nasson College office with special pains to point out on the wall sign in Lou's office that the college was located in Springvale, Maine. Lou holds a copy of the *Union Leader* and is wearing a blue business suit with a red tie. On his lapel is a button bearing the words "Liberal Lou." In the bubble quote, Lou states, "Finnegan, retract your editorial, or I'll make you pay…on my next visit to New Hampshire!" [7]

Lou's campaign problems were not limited to the *Union Leader's* jabs. He was welcomed to the Democratic Party, but his new colleagues were cautious. According to Lou, "I think the party was still lukewarm about me at the time. Many Democrats saw me as competition, and that took some years to get over." Despite the newspaper attacks and less-than-vigorous party support, Lou felt good about his election chances. "We had a first-class campaign – we thought we were going to win." The election effort felt good to Lou. It was gratifying to be back in politics as it was something that never left his blood. Even in the immediate wake of his 1982 gubernatorial primary loss to Sununu, it was suggested he run as a Democrat. Bill Moore, a pollster at the University of New Hampshire who later went to work for Gallup, wanted Lou to switch parties and run against Sununu but that wasn't remotely in the cards at the time. Four years later, a party switch and a new race were a reality.

Voters went to the polls on Tuesday, November 4th to decide New Hampshire's races for governor, the U.S. Senate and U.S. House of Representatives, along with the Fourth District Executive Council. The contest for the Executive Council proved to be the nail-biter. The winner was not decided until early in the morning of November 5, when the district's last votes from Derry were tallied. In what was deemed an upset, Earl Rinker defeated Lou D'Allesandro by 1406 votes, 22,926 to 21,250[8], or less than two percent. There was little doubt in Lou's mind that the *Union Leader's* incessant attacks on his out-of-state employment made the difference. In those days, the newspaper was still a force to be reckoned with and it was no friend of Lou's.

The aftermath of Lou's loss in 1986 was a lot easier to reconcile and adjust to than the gubernatorial primary defeats. For one thing, as the *Union Leader* was happy to often point out, Lou had a job as Nasson College's president. He hadn't had that luxury in his two races for governor. It was also his first election bid as a Democrat, and that change would require a few more adjustments.

The 1986 loss also provided a hint of things to come. During Lou's unsuccessful effort, he met Joe Biden, a senator from Delaware. Biden was first elected to the senate in 1972. At the time he was just shy of his thirtieth birthday, making him the sixth-youngest senator in U.S. history.[9] By 1986, Biden was in New Hampshire exploring the possibility of a run for president. Biden's contact with Lou and their ensuing friendship was part of a foundation that every presidential hopeful must lay in the Granite State if they hope to get off to a proper start in the primary season. Lou met Joe Biden's children, too. D'Allesandro also got a call from Biden after his loss to Rinker. The senator expressed his condolences on the defeat and encouraged D'Allesandro to play an active part in the Democratic Party. Lou was heartened by Biden's encouragement in the immediate wake of the 1986 defeat. Lou was upbeat, saying:

I think we came out of this election extremely optimistic about the future of the Democratic Party in New Hampshire and about the future of Lou D'Allesandro. We brought a message to the people that the people responded to in a broad philosophical sense.[10]

Whatever his level of encouragement in the days following the Fourth District Council election, the loss began a more than decade-long absence from state office-holding for D'Allesandro. That didn't mean Lou was completely uninvolved, just that his attention eventually turned to politics of the local variety. "All politics is local," a saying most often associated with former Speaker of the House Thomas "Tip" O'Neil, is especially true when you have three children in a school system.[11] In 1992, Lou was elected to a term on the Manchester School Board. Before he finished he would be elected to five consecutive two-year terms. "I had always been interested in the schools," observed Lou, "I saw that the schools were deteriorating. The grammar school on the west side of Manchester where we lived was being ignored."

Lou remembers that his children's elementary school used to hold an annual carnival to provide financial assistance to the school. "The school needed the money, it was falling apart," remembers Lou. Susan Wornick, who went on to a career in Boston-area television, was a radio personality in Manchester at the time and she hosted the carnivals. The school got a new principal, and the carnival and other activities like it disappeared. "It's the reason I first ran," notes Lou. "I felt the spirit of the school was reduced and that had to be reversed."

In retrospect Lou admits, "It was the toughest job I ever had. I gave them ten years of being out at meetings three to four nights a week." Lou worked on initiatives ranging from reorganized scheduling to school construction. On occasion it was as simple as pushing to get the schools properly cleaned. At one point the district outsourced the janitorial duties and the cleanliness of the building went downhill. The condition of the buildings was not the only problem inside the schools. "There was rancor surfacing in the schools, kids were bringing weapons to school, and bullying was an increasing problem," says D'Allesandro. "We formed a discipline committee and brought in resource officers."

Many of the efforts to address school issues brought only futility.

D'Allesandro smiles when he says, "It was great training for the senate." A number of projects Lou worked on never got off the ground. The class scheduling revisions Lou introduced were never implemented. The idea was simple: reduce the number of class changes to increase the amount of effective class time. But the teachers opposed the longer classes despite the positive impact on instruction time.

D'Allesandro's work on the school board and in other community capacities was creating a good deal of visibility. In 1997 he began a five-year stint as a host and producer of a Manchester Community Television show that examined a variety of issues. The format included interviews with a wide assortment of New Hampshire newsmakers. Before the television show, Lou spent three years as a Manchester radio talk show host. His radio program focused on exploring job opportunities and networking with the help of guest interviews. While Lou's community profile was on the rise, the *Union Leader's* grip on the hearts and minds of the Granite State's residents was on the decline. According to Lou, "at the time the paper was losing its ability to alter the populace." At the same time, national campaigns were starting to recognize that Lou D'Allesandro was an important resource to pursue. Lou was the sort of "person on the ground" that a national candidate needed in order to establish an effective base. Once Lou was elected to the New Hampshire Senate, a number of dynamics would come together quickly and make that conclusion an undeniable political reality in New Hampshire. With a first-in-the-nation primary, everything that happens in the Granite State is magnified in the nation's presidential sweepstakes when it arrives every four years.

CHAPTER 13

Senate Challenge

Democratic incumbent state Senator Ann Bourque decided not to run for reelection to the District 20 seat in 1994. Bourque, who had spent nearly a decade in New Hampshire politics, told the press that she wanted to spend more time with her family. The vacant seat attracted the attention of two Republicans, Richard Danais and David Letellier, and one Democrat, Lou D'Allesandro. Danais was a Manchester restaurateur and Letellier a chiropractor who was interested in certain reforms within his profession. The Manchester chiropractor said he would welcome a campaign against D'Allesandro if he made it through the Republican primary. "He's too liberal, more liberal than Ann Bourque ever was, and I think he's got more baggage." In response to Letellier's comment, D'Allesandro, who lived in the same Manchester ward as Letellier, noted, "It could be an easy campaign. We could yell at each other across the street." In the end, Letellier left his luggage at home and never entered the race.[1]

Lou got clearance from his boss Walter Peterson to run and made it to the general election uncontested. He hired a campaign manager from Londonderry named Beth Petrone, who had recently relocated from Connecticut where she had a career in information technology and finance. "She was the perfect campaign manager," says Lou with fond conviction. "Beth was in between jobs when we hired her. She was brilliant and had a natural political savvy. Her ideas set the stage for many campaigns to come; we are still using logos and art she designed. She had great political acumen."

Petrone's first challenge was the co-owner of the Dancing Bear Restaurant. Danais was also a real estate developer and a prominent Manchester Republican. The perennial political issue in the Granite State was once again front and center. Taxes, principally the "live free and die" state's disdain for a sales or income tax, was again a highlight in the campaign. Danais did his best to paint Lou as a big spender and the *Union Leader* was happy to assist in the effort. But as it turned out, public finances may not have been the pivotal issue in the race.

Weeks before the campaign's conclusion, Lou's campaign became aware of a criminal conviction of its opponent. Allegedly, the misdeed, a driving while under the influence charge (DWI), landed Danais in jail for a period of time. The D'Allesandro campaign didn't use the information but when an anonymous caller phoned into a Manchester radio show with the allegation, the D'Allesandro campaign got blamed for it. Lou's philosophy on the matter was simple: "We didn't have to use the information because we believed we were going to win the election. We ran as good a campaign as we could have possibly run, but the radio thing became a problem."[2]

The 20th Senate District, comprised of four wards of Manchester and the Town of Goffstown, was considered a relatively safe Democratic district. Goffstown, however, was a growing suburb and that was where the Republican votes were most abundant. Danais did his best to spin the DWI issue against D'Allesandro and the newspaper was happy to help. According to Lou, "the best thing the newspaper (*Union Leader*) could do for me was to ignore me." When voters finally went to the polls, Danais outran Lou 5756 to 4481. The result in Manchester was close, 3265 to 3015. The vote in Goffstown was not. Danais outpolled D'Allesandro by more than one thousand votes, 2491 to 1466.[3] Danais' popularity did not have the longevity usually associated with incumbent office holders. He would not face Lou D'Allesandro in another election, but Lou was still interested in winning the District 20 Senate seat. In four short years, D'Allesandro would be back with another campaign and another battle for the confidence of the district's voters.

Before Lou made another try for the senate, he ran and won a seat in the House of Representatives during the fall of 1996.[4] Twenty-five years and a wealth of experience separated his first term in the House from the one he took an oath for in January 1997. Not unlike his initial term there, the stay there would be short, a mere stopover in the end. Consistent with nearly all of his past experience, political change was only one of the adjustments to which Lou would need to adapt while completing his House term.

A year before Lou took his seat in the House, Walter Peterson left the presidency at Franklin Pierce for a job as president of the University of New Hampshire. Lou got along well enough with Peterson's replacement at Franklin Pierce; however, other circumstances soon interfered. Lou sought to discharge an employee he supervised for a lack of performance, but the academic dean intervened and the disagreement nearly resulted in blows. It soon became evident that the two men could not co-exist at the college. It was pretty straightforward according to Lou. "One of us could not stay and I was the easiest person to let go."

Suddenly Lou was out of the education field for the first time in more than a decade. Not unlike his exit from education in 1983, his career took an unexpected path. Of all the possible options, he found work in bus sales. When Lou was a freshman at UNH, he waited in a line to purchase his college textbooks, only to find out he was $50 short of what he needed to buy his first semester's books. With him in line was a fellow classmate he had just met. Joe Alosa generously loaned Lou the money to complete his purchase and the two became instant friends. Unfortunately for Joe, his father's untimely passing forced him to leave college and take the reins of the family company. Forty years later, Lou was welcomed aboard Patsy's Bus Company.

Joe sent Lou to Atlanta to learn the bus industry. Alosa sold Ford bus chassis to a number of different companies for various bus transportation needs. Lou convinced his new employer to broaden his market and include more moderately priced buses. Lou enjoyed great success and booked robust sales. Some of his accounts included the Manchester Airport Authority for their "park and fly" program and similarly purposed buses for Logan Airport services in Boston. For Lou, the key was designing a bus that fit the customer's budget. "I built a good business," says Lou. "Joe still gets comments about that salesman he had twenty years ago," he says with a smile.

Just as Lou was establishing a solid sales base with Patsy's, political opportunity came knocking again. Richard Danais, his former senate race opponent in fall 1994, announced he was not running for re-election in 1998.[5] Danais had been the subject of a recently concluded Attorney General's investigation connected to his involvement with the co-owner of a greyhound racing facility in Belmont. Danais was cleared of any criminal wrongdoing but the Attorney General did find the relationship "may have created a conflict of interest with respect to some of the matters he worked on."[6] With Danais gone, the District 20 picture had changed greatly.

Lou cruised through the Democratic primary unopposed. His general election rival, Tim Reiniger, was a newcomer and the Manchester Alderman swept every district precinct in defeating fellow Republican and House Majority Leader Bob Wheeler on his way to the Republican Party's nomination. By the time Reiniger faced Lou for the New Hampshire Senate, he had won three straights contests for his Manchester Alderman's seat. In his first race for that job, he upset Ann Bourque, who held an alderman post and the District 20 senate job simultaneously. Bourque's retirement from the senate coincided with her loss to Reiniger.[7]

The senate candidates were coming from very different places, both in experience and policy perspective. At the time, Lou was already a political veteran. According to the *Union Leader*, "D'Allesandro, 60, has endured an up-and-down career through a generation of the Granite State political scene." In contrast, Reiniger, 35, was a Manchester lawyer with only a fraction of the political races under his belt that the veteran D'Allesandro had participated in. The D'Allesandro – Reiniger race was closely watched since it had big implications in the battle for control of the senate. It was New Hampshire's key state contest at the time.

For Lou, one of the crucial policy differences with Reiniger involved education. D'Allesandro made his position clear in the October 7th edition of the *Union Leader*:

> *I think education has been underfunded," said D'Allesandro, who spent nearly 40 years in education as a teacher, coach and administrator. "The state has never adequately funded education, period, and it has never fulfilled its commitment.[8]*

Reiniger was less concerned about the funding of New Hampshire education than its reform. He saw the problem more in terms of a greater value for monies already appropriated rather than adding additional funding to the system. Reiniger wanted the state to address education and formulas by targeting funds to the communities in need. The Republican challenger also criticized D'Allesandro for positions he took as a Manchester School Board member, including the approval of a health survey for students that contained questions about sexual activity.[9]

While neither candidate supported any broad-based new taxation, Lou was able to get the jump on Reiniger by labeling him "Taxing Tim." As an alderman, Reiniger supported taxes for those attempting to do business in the Queen City. Lou was able to claim the high ground on taxes and assure the electorate that he was not an excessive spender.[10]

Whatever the debate about education or state finances, there was one category that Lou could lay unfettered claim to – experience. The Democratic House member had a clear advantage over his challenger in that category, and made it a clear part of his campaign. "I think I know what's going on," Lou told the *Union Leader*. "I think I have the respect of my peers." Lou was quick to point out specifics, whether it was electric rates or health care reform. "I've lowered electric rates for 20 years before Timmy came to New Hampshire," D'Allesandro told the newspaper while citing his involvement in the campaign for ratepayers' rights. He further informed the *Union Leader* reporter, "When there was a problem with health care in Manchester, the mayor came to me." That communication led to the formation of a health care task force.[11]

Lou's watershed 1998 race for the New Hampshire Senate occurred during a politically tumultuous time in the nation. Races across the country were hotly contested, and the D'Allesandro – Reiniger contest was no exception. Lou's senate race coincided with the country's mid-term 1998 Congressional elections. Banking on the impact of President Clinton's scandal with Monica Lewinsky and the growing calls for impeachment after the release of Independent Counsel Kenneth Starr's report, Republicans were hoping to gain seats in the House. That did not happen. When voters went to the polls on November 3rd, Republicans lost five seats to the Democrats in Congress, but still held a narrow majority. House Speaker

Newt Gingrich was a casualty of the discontent with his party and he was replaced by Congressman Dennis Hastert of Illinois.[12]

Things were not much different in New Hampshire. Incumbent Democratic Governor Jeanne Shaheen, a former New Hampshire state senator, easily defeated Republican challenger Jay Lucas by 66 to 31 percent.[13] Democrats gained control of the New Hampshire State Senate for the first time since 1912. The new majority senate party gained four seats in 1998 and accordingly held 13 of the 24 senate districts. Lou's Senate District 20 was one of them.[14] The Republican Party Chairman, Steve Duprey, said, "They ran one campaign for 24 districts, we tended to have 24 different campaigns." The Democratic Senate Chair, Jeff Woodburn, noted in his post-election remarks, "we have captured the center of the political dialogue." [15] Lou D'Allesandro would tend to agree. Moderate discourse on political issues that matter most to people was something Lou had made his hallmark for two-and-one-half decades and it paid off in the 1998 senate contest.

The highly contested race produced a predictably close result. Lou recalls, "I was nervous, but that's something that always goes along with elections." The campaign staffers and supporters, about one hundred strong, gathered at the Henry J. Sweeney American Legion Post to hear the results come in. The Manchester wards, Lou's stronghold, reported first so the final result ultimately hinged on Goffstown. In the end, D'Allesandro out-polled Reiniger 5974 to 5506. Reiniger took the Town of Goffstown 2249 to 1985, but Lou held sway in three of the four Manchester wards that were a part of Senate District 20. In Ward 10, Lou's home ward, he made his strongest showing, easily defeating Reiniger 1357 to 954, a 403-vote difference. These votes made up all but 65 of the total votes that separated the two candidates.[16]

"I was euphoric," recalls Lou. "I had not run in Goffstown in four years and it was a big test. I remember doing standouts in front of Sully's Market in downtown Goffstown. It was the only market on that side of town and we worked hard there." The senate victory was a big turning point for Lou. In many ways, it was both the culmination of a great deal of work and a large amount of political experience. "The win was a big deal," Lou notes. "Cards and congratulatory calls came in from all over, and that included presidential candidates, past and future." D'Allesandro was on the precipice of putting all his gains to work in one facet of a varied career he would ultimately hold onto longer than any other. The result was destined to reverberate like nothing else he had ever experienced.

CHAPTER 14

Entering the National Scene

Bill Clinton was huddled in a room with twelve of his closest New Hampshire supporters at Manchester's Radisson Hotel. All of the shades were drawn and the hallways were guarded by dogs and Secret Service agents. Clinton was in the midst of turmoil over the White House sex scandal that continued without abatement after the 1998 mid-term elections. The president needed some encouragement and he came to New Hampshire for it. Fresh out of his first state senate win, Lou was a part of that meeting. "It was like a booster club," Lou recalls. "It was good for him and it was good for us."

It wasn't the newly elected senator's first brush with Clinton and it would not be his last either. Lou and Pat attended both of Clinton's inaugurations. They and other New Hampshire supporters were conspicuously rewarded when the ball for the Granite State's attendees was combined with that of the President's home state of Arkansas. Pat remembers it as "the ball with the greatest entertainment, the one everyone wanted to attend." D'Allesandro was invited or summoned to the White House on a number of occasions during the Clinton administration. Bill Cashin, the longest-serving alderman in Manchester history, had close ties to Clinton. Cashin represented Lou's home ward and helped pave the way for Lou in enhancing his connection to the president. Lou got invited to an education bill signing at the White House and had an opportunity to speak to Clinton briefly. The New Hampshire Senate President sent Lou to Washington in 1998 to meet with Housing and Urban Development Secretary Andrew Cuomo, when a low-income housing issue in Keene needed to be addressed. Lou had been an early supporter of Mario

Cuomo, Andrew's father. Lou would have been on the front lines if Mario's rousing speech at the 1984 Democratic Convention had ever translated into a campaign for the presidency.

There were lighter moments too, when the D'Allesandros attended Christmas parties at the Clinton White House. Lou has fond memories of taking his youngest daughter, Christina, to one of those festive gatherings – it was Christina who had the keenest interest in politics out of the three D'Allesandro children. But Lou's first term in the senate was not all fun and games. Although his party had gained control of the upper chamber, there was no guarantee it would translate into a meaningful committee assignment.

The new Senate President in 1998 was Clesson "Junie" Blaisdell, a Democrat from Keene and the former finance chairman. Lou knew Blaisdell fairly well, as both men had connections to the sporting world. As a former football and basketball coach, Lou knew the Senate President owned a sporting goods store and refereed basketball games. It was Blaisdell's days wearing the stripes that had brought the two men in contact, sometimes confrontationally if Lou was irritated by a call on the court. While Blaisdell buried the freshman senator on some meaningless committees, he did give Lou one assignment of significance: an appointment as an alternate member to the New England Board of Higher Education. The Board was a tool to promote education opportunities and served the entire New England region. Lou joined his friend Walter Peterson, who was the board's chairman. It greatly broadened Lou's political base and his relevance on the national political stage. In time he would succeed to the chairmanship.

There were other impactful events that occurred during Lou's first term in the senate. First, Blaisdell died halfway through the term.[1] His passing not only left a vacancy with respect to his senate duties but also an open director's seat on the Federal Home Loan Bank of Boston, an important resource for the regulation of home credit. The Bank, which continues today, is made up of hundreds of member banks throughout the New England region and is a source of credit for its member banks. In turn, the member banks provide New England homeowners with a reliable source of mortgage financing. The Federal Home Loan Bank in Boston and its counterparts in other cities are regulated by a bureau of the

U.S. Treasury Department.[2] At the time of Blaisdell's passing, and Lou's appointment to the bank's board, the 2000 presidential campaign was well underway. Soon Al Gore came a-calling to Manchester's Ward 10 and visited its most politically experienced resident, Lou D'Allesandro.

Lou had known the vice president since the days Gore competed with Bill Clinton for the Democratic nomination in 1988. Gore slept at the D'Allesandro home during a stop in New Hampshire. Lou remembers what a well-mannered gentleman the future vice president was. "After Pat cooked us all dinner and we finished, he got up and cleared the table, He didn't have one ounce of pretense. The next morning, we found that he had made his own bed." But that was 1988, and eventually the senator from Tennessee's bid for the White House turned into eight years as Bill Clinton's vice president when Gore chose not to run for president in 1992. Now he was seeking to catapult his steady leadership in that role to the nation's top political prize.

Lou took the vice president everywhere. It was a kaleidoscope of varied places that had become the stomping ground of presidential candidates eager to win the nation's first primary and provide their young candidacy instant credibility and supremacy. With those stakes firmly in mind, off went the vice president and Lou. They went to Pappy's Pizza, long a staple of Lou's campaign efforts, where the senator had on a number of occasions waited on tables, bussed them after the diners finished, and washed dishes in an effort to truly get to know the people of District 20. There was an obligatory stop at the Red Arrow Diner, which by then had become a traditional place to visit by those seeking the country's highest office. Lou took Al Gore to the Back Room, Manchester's largest restaurant, and to Chez Vachon, a French restaurant where Bill Clinton had enjoyed dining on poutine and *patates frites*.

For his efforts, Lou was not only in attendance at the convention that nominated Gore, but he got some first-class treatment while in Los Angeles. One of the functions was a party at Magic Johnson's house. For a guy who was once as involved in basketball as much as Lou was, that was special. "It was like visiting a shrine," remembers Lou. "There was memorabilia and awards everywhere, it was a basketball mecca."

Nice treatment at the convention was not the only reward for Lou. It was at that time he was summoned to the Blair House in Washington, the president's guest house, to be vetted for Blaisdell's open seat on the Federal Home Loan Bank of Boston. There was competition for the job, but after a meeting with the vice president's staff, Lou learned he had secured the appointment. It was a significant advancement for the first-term Granite State senator and established Lou more securely as an important participant on the national stage. Lou spent three fruitful years as a bank board member and before he was through, he was elected the vice chairman of the board.[3]

All of the national politics and exposure were fine and well, but none of it would matter much if Lou didn't secure his seat in the New Hampshire State Senate. Al Gore's campaign wasn't the only one Lou had to pay attention to in 2000; there was his own as well. Lou was unopposed for his party's nomination but in the general election he faced Bruce F. Hunter, a Goffstown Republican. Lou was the clear favorite in the race, but Goffstown was the center of the district's Republican vote and Hunter was expected to do well there. While Lou lost in Goffstown by 3779 to 3442, the four Manchester wards more than made up the difference. The total vote count was in Lou's favor, 10,177 to 7,922. While outpolled there, D'Allesandro's showing in Goffstown was encouraging since he was closing the gap where the Republicans needed votes the most.[4] Some commentators thought Lou should have beaten Hunter by a wider margin – but with a solid eleven percent win, Lou was moving on to his second term. The man he backed for the presidency had far greater complications in the days immediately following the election.

The 2000 presidential election became one of high drama when the decision between Gore and Bush hung in the balance for 36 days after the election like the famous chads from the state of Florida's paper ballots. The Democratic electoral strategy was simple, win Florida and win it all. But something went wrong – and the margin in Florida became so thin it would take the U.S. Supreme Court to figure the whole thing out. A dizzying process of recounts (machine and manual), deadlines, and extended deadlines ended on December 12, 2000. The U.S. Supreme Court, in a 5-4 ruling, ended the Florida recount process by declaring George Bush the winner by 537 votes as certified by Florida Secretary of State Katherine Harris on November 26th. Gore formally conceded the election the next day.[5] One of the Court's dissenters, Justice John Paul Stevens, wrote, "Although we may never know with complete certainty the identity of the winner of this year's Presidential election, the identity of the loser is perfectly clear, it is the Nation's confidence in the judge as an impartial guardian of the rule of law." [6] The election was the closest since 1876 and represented the fourth time in history where the Electoral College winner did not obtain a majority of the popular vote – the fifth time occurred in 2016.[7]

In the wake of the presidential election but before the Supreme Court decided whether Bush or Gore had won, Lou met with President Clinton at Manchester's Merrimack Spa Restaurant. The two men dissected the election results. "We agreed that it came down to an allocation of resources," observed Lou. "The strategy became all or nothing with Florida. Neither I nor the president saw that as sound." The Gore campaign diverted personnel from New Hampshire and Gore's home state of Tennessee. In the process, Gore lost both states and 15 Electoral College votes. New Hampshire with its 4 votes would have alone been enough to swing the victory to Gore.

Lou made other visits after the election, including one to Tennessee where he dined with Al and Tipper Gore. After dinner, the Gores gave Lou a tour of Nashville, where the Granite State senator met Bill Purcell, the city's mayor. The two men became friends. Naturally, the conversation while Lou was in Nashville was dominated by the election. It was only days after Gore's concession and the sting of the historic outcome was still very fresh. "We talked about the election," recalls Lou. "We talked about some people who just didn't deliver; it was a recap of sorts. It wasn't a discussion filled with animosity, just a sifting of facts."

D'Allesandro was in a rather unique position to assess the 2000 presidential election and that wasn't limited to a debriefing of Gore and Clinton. The Supreme Court became the ultimate player in a presidential election that tested the Constitutional fiber of the United States and the rule of law. The stakes were so high that even veteran law clerks of the nation's highest court were surprised by the political overtones that surrounded *Bush v. Gore*.[8] The case, perhaps more than any other decided, proved the persuasive power of the institution and on December 12, 2000, the decision put to rest one the nation's most intense political controversies since *Marbury v. Madison* (which established the principle of judicial review in the first place).[9] A divided court decided *Bush v. Gore*, and shortly after the decision was announced, Lou got to visit an old friend, David Souter, one of the four justices in the dissent. The meeting brought the men back to days when they concurrently served New Hampshire state government. Their common friend, Warren Rudman, appointed Souter Deputy Attorney General in 1971 when Rudman was the Granite State's Attorney General. Lou was on the Executive Council while Souter was Deputy Attorney General and the two men got to know each other. Five years later, Souter ascended to the top job in the Attorney General's office.[10]

After the ruling in *Bush v. Gore*, Lou had the unique chance to meet personally with Justice Souter in his Washington office. Souter wrote a separate dissenting opinion in which his fellow dissenting justices (Breyer, Stevens and Ginsburg) agreed with the exception of Part III of Souter's opinion.[11] That portion of Souter's dissenting opinion focused on the main thrust of the majority – that there were disparities in how various Florida counties were assessing voter's intentions as they recounted ballots "exhibiting identical physical characteristics (such as hanging or dimpled chads)." The majority concluded that there was no effective way to conduct a recount of the undervotes, (those for which no presidential choice was recorded by a machine) within the deadline for certifying presidential electors, December 18th.

Souter disagreed. Firstly, he estimated the undervote to be about 60,000, an uncontradicted representation made by counsel for Gore, not the 170,000 estimated by one of Florida's state Supreme Court justices. Souter believed there was time to remand the case to the Florida Supreme Court with instructions to "…establish uniform standards, for evaluating the several types of ballots that have prompted differing." Souter admitted getting the standards established and the ballots assessed in six days "… would be a tall order." Nonetheless, he concluded, "There is no justification for denying the state the opportunity to try to count all the disputed ballots now."[12] According to Lou, Souter's rationale was characteristic of the reasoned, pragmatic approach that was a hallmark of his friend while the two cut their teeth in Granite State government. "Souter is a decent and honorable guy," Lou notes unequivocally. "He had deep concerns for the country when the decision came down." The change Lou experienced in late 2000 was not confined to the federal government.

Lou's responsibilities in the New Hampshire Senate were also marked by a change in party control. In 2000 the Republicans regained control of the senate. The new Senate President was Arthur Klemm, who happened to be a friend of Lou's.[13] Despite the men being in different parties, Lou got a key appointment as Ways and Means chairman.[14] It was both unorthodox, and at the same time emblematic of Lou's political career. It was an example of Lou working the center as a moderate who was passionate about solving problems. In an ironic twist, Lou actually received better treatment from the Republican senate leadership in his second term than from the Democratic leadership in his first.

One of the accomplishments of Lou's second term was tied to an expansion of gaming in New Hampshire. It is an issue that has followed much of his career in the senate. In his second term, he supported the licensing of slot machines when the tax revenues generated were invested in education. The mantra became the rather clumsy slogan, "Slots for Tots." Lou's record on gaming has never involved open-ended support. In the 2017 legislative session, he opposed a bill referred to in an uncannily similar way as the one-armed bandit legislation. "Keno for Kindergarten" was the modern moniker for the state's latest gaming-for-education statute. To Lou, the Keno legislation represented an untoward gambling initiative. "I thought it was the least responsible expansion of gaming. It will produce no jobs and it is a highly addictive form of gambling."

There were many years between the slot machines and Keno and many challenges along the way, but as early as his second term, Lou was making a mark in the New Hampshire senate. A third term would set the stage for some big things. Despite all of the years and changes already behind the Manchester Democrat, the most dramatic days were still ahead. The core of Lou D'Allesandro's political destiny loomed just ahead. There were both significant legislative issues facing New Hampshire and politics at the highest level in the Manchester Democrat's path.

CHAPTER 15

Education Reform and Senate Doings

Lou's second term in the New Hampshire Senate was shaped in part by an opportunity only indirectly related to politics. Lou was selected as a Caroline Gross Fellow and received a scholarship to attend a program at Harvard University's Kennedy School of Government. The selection process involved a nomination followed by competitive interviews before the New Hampshire Charitable Foundation. The District 20 senator was honored to be the foundation's choice to participate in the month-long course that examined political trends and how issues impact campaign decision-making.[1]

Networking was also a big part of the Kennedy School program. It was during that month in Cambridge that Lou met Lou Papan, a California assemblyman and the chairman of the Assembly's Banking Committee. It didn't take the men long to form a bond and a lifelong friendship. "He was a big deal in California," Lou notes. "Lou Papan founded a bank and had a long and influential career in the California Assembly." As it turned out, Papan was known as the "Dean of the California Assembly" for his twenty years of service.[2] It was a title his new friend would eventually earn in the New Hampshire Senate for a similar term of service.

For ten of Papan's years in the Assembly, he chaired the powerful Rules Committee. He was known as "the enforcer" because of his ability to cobble together votes on important issues. His other nickname had little to do with his political acumen. His penchant to habitually speed back and forth between his home in Millbrae and Sacramento earned him the moniker "Lead Foot Lou." He also earned a multitude of speeding tickets from the California Highway Patrol. In his defense, his motivation was most often to get home quickly to spend time with his son, who suffered from a rare congenital condition that took his life at age 21 in 1981.[3] When Papan himself died at age 78 in 2007, memorials poured in, including tributes from Governor Arnold Schwarzenegger and fellow assemblymen. But Lou D'Allesandro agreed that one of the Assembly staffers, Alex Tourse, said it best, "He was one of those rare politicians who would advocate publicly what he believed privately." [4]

It was that sort of statecraft that the two Lou's were exposed to as they formed their friendship at Harvard University. The instructor introduced case studies and scenarios to the class. Lou remembers that one area of study involved the case for equity in wage payments to women and minorities. Lou decided to do a little field study – to walk among the black community. One of the other attendees was a black college administrator. Her husband was the former mayor of Seattle. The couple belonged to a black Baptist church in Cambridge. Lou went to their church not knowing entirely what to expect. "It was an attempt to heal differences between the white and black communities, a time for understanding," Lou recalls. D'Allesandro reported his experiences back to the class. "I thought it was interesting, especially coming from the Catholic Church. I had never seen anything like it. There was so much interaction between the congregation and the preacher. I recommended that the other students in the program try it."

The program opened Lou's eyes in a number of ways, some social and others more related to the nuts and bolts of government. California had already experienced the deregulation of electricity by the time D'Allesandro met Lou Papan. Things didn't go entirely well in California with the experience and D'Allesandro was able to pick up lessons and potential pitfalls as New Hampshire faced similar issues. But the seminal legislation facing New Hampshire in 2001 was education reform. This wasn't something entirely new; it was a problem facing the Granite State in the aftermath of a couple of decisions impacting education financing handed down by the New Hampshire Supreme Court.

In 1971, the California Supreme Court decided the Serrano case that held disparity in school funding among that state's school districts was not acceptable.[5] The California decision touched off similar challenges in other states nationwide. The first challenge in New Hampshire came in the early 1980s. A suit brought by the Town of Claremont and four other less fortunate communities sought to establish a greater role for the state in education funding.[6] Governor Sununu hired John Augenblick, a consultant who derived a formula to provide additional assistance to poorer school districts, and the suit was dropped. The Augenblick formula was not sufficient to solve the problem. (New Hampshire ranked dead last among the states in state aid to education, even after Augenblick.)[7]

By the early 1990s, Claremont and other similarly situated communities and school districts were once again in financial trouble. *Claremont v. the Governor of New Hampshire* was brought on behalf of five school districts to insure an equitable amount of state education funding for all the state's school districts. In 1993, the New Hampshire Supreme Court ruled that the state constitution imposed a duty upon the state to provide an adequate education to each child in the state and guarantee funding for the same.[8] Four years later the New Hampshire high court ruled in *Claremont II*, a second suit which sought to better define the state's role in education funding. In the simplest terms, *Claremont II* required that the state define a threshold deemed an "adequate education" and pay for it with state-raised tax dollars.[9] Lou sets out the recurring legislative challenge: "It is the primary responsibility of the legislature to tax in an equal and proportional manner while providing every student a free and appropriate education." If the theory sounds simple and fair, its implementation has been anything but that.

Since 1997, state aid to education has taken the form of a series of funding mechanisms including a new state-wide property tax. The new property tax is used to fund a part of the state's school funding obligation. After a short experiment which provided a tool to divert some of the property tax revenue from richer communities to poorer ones, the state-wide property tax is now spent on education funding in the community where the tax dollars are raised, either in current years or for future needs should a surplus be accumulated. Because the state-wide property tax is not by itself sufficient to fund the state's schools, the state provides communities an "adequacy payment" which is funded from a percentage of state revenues derived from a business profits tax, an enterprise tax, and the lottery.[10]

Missing from the discussion was the notion of either a state income or sales tax. Either of those levies was and is political heresy in the "Live Free or Die" state. Freedom from those taxes, at least in a direct sense, is part of the state's creed. Any serious office holder or candidate knows the peril of even mentioning the words. According to Lou, "It was a culture created by the *Union Leader*. There is pride taken that we run the state without an income or sales tax." The newspaper required candidates to take the "no tax" pledge biennium after biennium as each election cycle came and went. When Lou ran for governor he refused to take the pledge. While he had no plan to introduce either tax, he simply objected to the newspaper's requirement. "It may have cost me the election," says D'Allesandro.

By 1999, only two years after *Claremont II*, the state was once again in crisis as it faced new difficulties in meeting its education funding responsibilities. Over the winter and spring months of that year, a House bill was hammered out that met the revenue requirements in a number of ways. The proposed legislation included the use of tobacco fund settlement proceeds due the state and an increase in tobacco taxes. HB117 was sent to conference and Lou D'Allesandro was a member of the Senate Conference Committee.

Lou had real issues with the use of tobacco taxes or tobacco settlement funds for schools. The money was intended to be used specifically for tobacco education, to lessen the impact of tobacco use on the health of New Hampshire residents and save lives. Using those monies to meet the state's school funding responsibilities was a contrivance. Lou's position was a major problem for the governor.

Jeanne Shaheen, today New Hampshire's senior U.S. senator, was then beginning her second term as New Hampshire's governor in early 1999. She needed the education funding crisis abated and the House bill was her best chance of doing that. If anyone thought it was possible, Lou's position on the tobacco money might have gotten him removed from the Conference Committee, but that was not in the cards. Lou's security as a Conference Committee member just made the problem all the more acute. He had the full confidence of and a close friendship with Junie Blaisdell, the Senate President. D'Allesandro wasn't going anywhere.

So the Senate Conference Committee met in Room 123 of the State House's main floor. Down the hall, their House counterparts took up their position in Room 100. Back and forth, a shuttle diplomacy ensued as the particulars of the joint conference bill were negotiated. But the tobacco money still troubled Lou and the governor knew it was a big hurdle in solving a very serious problem. A meeting was arranged between Lou and Governor Shaheen. Room 123 is a three-room suite, comprised of a conference room, a reception area and a private office. The governor and the senator met one-on-one in the private office. It was a showdown of sorts – one based on issues, not personalities. Shaheen let Lou know how much she needed the bill. There was little disguising her anxiety about it. Lou remembers the governor having tears in her eyes. "I recognized it was a make-or-break situation," says Lou. "I knew how important it was for kids and education. It was also important for Jeanne and she was a fellow Democrat and a friend. I pledged my vote."

Education funding took a great deal of effort in 1999, and Governor Shaheen signed the bill on April 29, 1999.[11] Not much has changed in ensuing years. One of the primary components for funding education in the Granite State was established in the 1999 law. The statute created an Education Trust Fund, which Lou calls a "phony fund." The so-called trust fund in fact contains no reserves or trust funds at all. It is merely a conduit to receive a matrix of revenues passed through the general fund to meet state aid to education. As a result, it is not distinct from the state's general fund revenues. For Lou, one of the solutions to the state's ever-present need for earmarked education revenues was gaming.

By 2001, school-funding solutions were still being sought by beleaguered state legislators. Lou used his leadership position as Ways and Means Chairman to guide brainstorming sessions to develop new and re-organized revenue sources. He set up weekly discussions with the governor, other key Democrats and a professional mediation team, all in an effort to arrive at a fair method to raise the state's share of education funding, which at the time approached $900 million annually. Lou's position was summed up in a *Concord Monitor* article from April 2001. "State-controlled gambling, not a hodgepodge of business taxes, should be the next step." The article continued:

"I think that's baloney," said D'Allesandro, when asked whether a mix of business taxes would raise enough money. "We need a big hit, and in my opinion gaming is the big hit."

A majority of New Hampshire residents support expanded gambling, he said. As long as the state controls it, gambling is "less repulsive" than any other proposals and should be considered an option, D'Allesandro said.

How to frame a gambling proposal is the real issue, he said.[12]

The forms of gaming that Lou sought to supplement education funding – casino and video gambling – have never been implemented in the Granite State. Instead, the state has been content to limit its experiment in casino-like gaming. That has taken the form of Las Vegas-themed nights run by charitable organizations. Nonprofits are allowed to conduct up to ten such nights a year.[13] While this may sound well-intentioned and altruistic, Lou is not so sure. First, he notes that these operations tap only a fraction of the potential revenue that could be raised for education if the industry was able to create well-regulated facilities in the state. Moreover, Lou believes the charitable model has created a well-entrenched system of operators who do more to meet their own profit expectations than either the interests of the charities they serve or the state. The professional gaming operators make the task of conducting a casino night easy for the nonprofit groups.[14] With that ease comes a cost – the diversion of most of the dollars to the operators and not to either the charity or state coffers. It has gotten to the point where the operators profiting from charitable gaming have their own lobby opposed to the expansion of gaming in New Hampshire. Recently, Lou joined a majority of legislators who killed a bill that sought to permit an increase in the maximum bets for charitable gaming events from four dollars to ten.

If there is one sure bet in New Hampshire, it's that the challenge of funding the state's schools will continue as it has for all the years Lou D'Allesandro has spent in the state senate. While it may not be the only challenge the Manchester Democrat has faced during his two decades in the senate, it has been the one dominant controversy that has produced his most sincere efforts. If the task of properly funding the state's schools was a constant from the beginning of Lou's legislative career, his own political relevance was on the verge of taking a dramatic turn as he entered his third term in the New Hampshire Senate. Great changes were in the offing.

The National Spotlight Burns Brighter

Lou's visibility on the national political stage had been growing for some time, but in November 2003 it exploded with a single newspaper article. Mark Leibovich, a writer for the *Washington Post*, was working on a series of reports about the all-important New Hampshire presidential primary. On Tuesday, November 25, 2003, Leibovich's column "Voter's Block" appeared in the *Post*. The story reverberated not only across the country in newspapers large and small, but around the world as well.

Democratic presidential hopefuls had been soliciting Lou's support for months. Leibovich announced the New Hampshire State Senator's endorsement and the world took note. The article not only declared which candidate would get D'Allesandro's political support but made clear D'Allesandro's importance in the presidential primary process. Leibovich started his piece, "There are times, when the big dogs start calling one after another, that Lou D'Allesandro must realize how vital he is to the democratic process." With Leibovich's write-up there was no hiding where Lou fit in. Now it was made clear that presidential candidates needed him. Their operatives inquired about his support and courted his coveted endorsement. In Leibovich's words, Lou is, "…a very important guy – a kingmaker."

The response to the Leibovich story was swift and strong. If the term had been in use during the early days of the new millennium, Lou's political importance in the presidential selection process would have been deemed to have "gone viral." According to the New Hampshire

Democrat, "The reaction was unbelievable, I heard from people all over the country. There was an avalanche of notes and emails from friends and politicians." Lou is quick to point out that it was easy to let all the attention go to your head. "You have to make a point to stay humble through all of it," Lou noted. The senator kids that his wife may disagree how successful he was with his sense of humility.

In 2003, as in other presidential races, Lou had a big decision to make. The Democratic field was stocked with candidates eager to take on George Bush and vindicate the party after the dramatic loss in the historic 2000 election. Contenders included Massachusetts Senator John Kerry, Senator John Edwards of North Carolina, and Connecticut Senator Joe Lieberman. There was also Missouri Congressman Dick Gephardt and Vermont Governor Howard Dean. Dean, who lacked name recognition, was the first to throw his hat in the ring by forming a presidential exploratory committee on May 21, 2002, nearly two years before the New Hampshire primary. In September 2003, more than a year after Dean's exploratory committee was formed, four-star general Wesley Clark, a native of Little Rock, Arkansas, announced his run for president in his hometown.[1]

Characteristic of his method in all presidential primary races, Lou took his time evaluating the field in 2003. He has been criticized for the length of time he employs to pick a candidate, mostly because the delay has the consequence of getting D'Allesandro a lot more attention from the national candidates and their campaigns. Lou doesn't see it that way. "I have a serious responsibility, and that's the way I take it," he notes. "I'm careful in determining just who to endorse." One political observer, who has worked with a variety of candidates and understands the drill well, mentioned Lou in his book on the 2004 race. Walter Shapiro, in *One-Car Caravan*, wrote, "Every time I come to New Hampshire with a presidential contender, a closed meeting with D'Allesandro is an enviable part of the process."[2] Private meetings are not the only part of the approach. There are bus tours, phone calls with the candidates, visits to the D'Allesandros Manchester home, and parties hosted by Lou and Pat.

In 2003, the contest for Lou's support really came down to two candidates, Dick Gephardt and John Edwards. Lou first met Gephardt when the Congressman ran for president in 1988. The two men developed some chemistry and shared similar philosophies. They kept in touch over the years and Gephardt was a serious consideration for Lou's favor in the 2004 race. Lou was candid when he admitted to Leibovich that he had, for all intents and purposes, narrowed his choice to Gephardt and Edwards as long as five months before the *Post* reporter's article ran. He told Leibovich that he still entertained the inquiries of all the Democratic candidates despite his early thoughts on the field. "I did it as a courtesy," Lou explained to Leibovich. D'Allesandro further justified his position to the reporter, "I want to be helpful to every Democrat." [3]

The two-man race for Lou's support was ultimately decided largely by a philosophy that recognized the widening gulf in America between the wealthy and privileged and those who struggled every day to get by. It was a recurrent theme that Edwards articulated, and according to Lou, "He articulated it very well." So well that Edwards captured the imagination of Democrats at their convention in July 2004 with his well-praised "Two Americas" speech made as the party's vice-presidential nominee. [4] But months before that, and in the days leading up to the New Hampshire primary, there were other factors that Edwards' campaign was able to exploit for Lou's support.

The Edwards campaign, knowing D'Allesandro's affinity for basketball, had one of the game's legends lobby the New Hampshire pol. Dean Smith, who played and coached at Kansas, was basketball royalty. Smith's coach at Kansas was Phog Allen, the most famous student of the game's inventor, James Naismith. The Hall of Famer went on to a thirty-five-year career at basketball powerhouse University of North Carolina, where Smith coached one of the NBA's best, Michael Jordan. [5] Smith supported Edwards, and it would have been difficult to think of a better basketball ambassador to reach out to Lou D'Allesandro. If there was a closer, however, it was Elizabeth Edwards. Like D'Allesandro, Mrs. Edwards was an Italian-American who struck a chord with Lou. "I got very close to Elizabeth and we maintained a friendship," Lou warmly recalls. "People were drawn to her. You could see how well-liked she was, she could relate easily wherever she went." Lou was won over. On October 30, 2003, over a conference call with Edwards and fifteen reporters, Lou announced that the North Carolina Senator, in the words of Leibovich, "(was) the winner of the 2003 D'Allesandro primary." Edwards quipped during the conference call, "We're gonna be such a good team." Lou explained his choice, "They're all outstanding candidates, but I feel the most comfortable with his ideas. He's a fresh face, and you need that." [6]

Unfortunately for Edwards, a win in the D'Allesandro primary did not mean a win in the 2004 New Hampshire primary. That distinction belonged to John Kerry, senator from bordering Massachusetts. Kerry took thirty-eight percent of the New Hampshire Democratic vote, followed by Dean with a twenty-six percent share. Clark and Edwards each had twelve percent. [7] Lou was with Edwards in a New Hampshire hotel when the disappointing returns came in. Lou believes that Kerry and Dean had big geographical advantages over the Southerner. According to Lou, "The electorate didn't have anything against Edwards in particular but the voters weren't quite as tuned into his message."

While Edwards did not get the start he wanted, the strength he showed during the primary season was a factor in him being added to the Democratic ticket as Kerry's running mate. Lou met Kerry during the New Hampshire primary at Grand Slam Pizza, where they boarded a trolley for a tour of Manchester. The two men got along well enough and Lou lobbied the Massachusetts Senator on behalf of Edwards. Lou was also able to use contacts he made while campaigning for Edwards in other states to bring the case for Edwards as a vice presidential running mate to Kerry.

The Kerry-Edwards ticket didn't succeed in 2004, but Edwards' problems were about to go far beyond the failed election. When the difficulties came, D'Allesandro felt them personally. Lou's closeness to Elizabeth Edwards is one of the greatest reasons for Lou's deep disappointment when John Edwards fell from grace after the scandal of his affair with a campaign videographer broke in 2008. [8] With a good deal of despair, Lou admits, "He had the greatest line of BS of anyone I ever met." The clean-cut guy and former athlete had another side. Today, D'Allesandro will tell you that Edwards let him down. "It was the greatest disappointment in politics that I ever suffered. I felt personally betrayed."

There is little doubt that Lou's friendship with Elizabeth Edwards made the sting of the scandal all the more palpable. Elizabeth's battle with cancer, fought concurrently with the damaging revelations about her husband, made the circumstances even more devastating. Mrs. Edwards first learned about a breast tumor the day after John Kerry and her husband lost the presidential election to George Bush and Dick Cheney in November 2004.[9] Mrs. Edwards courageously fought the cancer into remission, but the cancer came back in spring 2007 while her husband was once again on the hunt for the presidency. This time the cancer spread, and while it was treatable, Mrs. Edwards revealed that it was no longer curable.[10] She played a dominant role in her husband's campaigns, as one of his closest advisers. Despite her illness, his campaign and her role in it continued. In 2008 Edwards lost the South Carolina primary and that signaled an end to his hopes for the party's nomination.[11]

In August of the same year, the admission of his affair with a campaign videographer all but finished his political career. Lou supported Mrs. Edwards throughout her joint ordeals. He wondered how she stayed married to Edwards. She was candid with Lou. "I'm going to die," admitted Elizabeth Edwards, "and he's the father of my children." Mrs. Edwards was once asked in an interview by Oprah Winfrey why she continued to support her husband after the first reports of his affair surfaced in 2006 and after she urged him to protect their family and end the campaign when those revelations broke. Mrs. Edwards responded, "Being sick meant a number of things to me. One is that my life is going to be less long, and I didn't want to spend it fighting." Lou stayed close to Elizabeth Edwards until her death from cancer on December 7, 2010 at age 61.[12] For Lou it was a moment of great sadness and one that fundamentally changed his view of politics.

The Edwards experience profoundly changed D'Allesandro. "The longer I'm in the business, the more I see the flaws," says Lou. "It's a pretty awful business and it can destroy you and your family." The way D'Allesandro sees it, one's moral compass must always trump party politics. He laughs when he recalls the advice a perennial New Hampshire political operative gave him. The man was blatant: "Lou, you should probably never run for politics again because people don't like you." That was many elections ago and today Lou knows that the relationships he has forged with the voters he serves and the more moderate members of both parties have never been more important. "I sought the Senate presidency once," notes Lou. But a leadership role in the upper chamber wasn't and isn't in the cards for the Manchester Democrat. "I'm not partisan enough," Lou boasts. He sees the polarization that is an undeniable part of today's politics as a fundamental hindrance. He's proud to call a number of moderate Republican senators friends. "While we aren't always going to agree," says Lou, "we are always going to talk."

While Lou may have taken on a more realistic attitude in the wake of the 2004 election, he still maintained hope for change. It's what keeps him on the front lines of Democratic politics. As the Edwards drama was unfolding, a new presidential race invaded the Granite State. The Bush years were over and there was a new player on the Democratic stage. In the words of Mark Leibovich, "the big dogs were calling," – again.[13]

CHAPTER 17

Relationship Politics

When the 2008 presidential campaign began to percolate, Lou was done with John Edwards and the rest of the country was not far behind. The Democratic primary race, even in its early stages, seemed to be between U.S. Senators Barack Obama of Illinois and Hillary Clinton of New York. While there were others in the mix besides Edwards, they were long shots even in the early polling. With the exception of Edwards, all the serious candidates got a look from D'Allesandro.

Lou took a liking to Bill Richardson, the governor of New Mexico. To Lou, Richardson was a down-to-earth guy. "I could talk to him about anything; he was humble in his approach to the primary." The two men have continued to talk and keep in touch with each other until this day. "He was President Clinton's ambassador to the United Nations and the U.S. Energy Secretary," notes Lou. "Bill demonstrated a strong foreign policy knowledge in the primary." [1] The D'Allesandros hosted a coffee at their Manchester home for Richardson and were delighted to do it. The one and only drawback in giving his endorsement to the New Mexico governor was related to the probability of Richardson's success. Lou saw a formidable uphill battle for Richardson in the 2008 field. "He just wasn't quite as electable as the top two candidates," D'Allesandro admits. "I had to be candid about that."

D'Allesandro was also courted by Joe Biden. Lou and Pat planned a house party for Biden, but it never came off because the Delaware senator's plane was delayed on its way to Manchester. Lou's connection to Biden and his family had a long history by the advent of the 2008 primary season. Biden's sons, Beau and Hunter once sported tee shirts advertising one of Lou's campaigns. Beau succumbed to brain cancer in 2015 after a two-year struggle. He was 46.[2] Lou gave an address honoring his friend on the floor of the New Hampshire Senate.

In 2007, Biden marched with Lou in Manchester's St. Patrick's Day Parade. As the two men made their way along the parade route, they were suddenly rushed by a man waiting on the side of the street. Startled at first, they eventually discovered that the man wanted to let Biden know he had been acquainted with Biden's first wife. Neilla Biden, along with the couple's daughter Naomi, was killed in a car accident while Christmas shopping on December 18, 1972. The two Biden boys were also in the car at the time but survived with serious injuries.[3] Nine months after the parade, Lou was on his way to the Biden home in Delaware. He was invited to a December meeting to discuss ways to improve relations between Cuba and the United States with Biden and his staff.

Biden's bid for the presidency in 2008 wasn't going any better than his attempt two decades earlier. It was pretty clear, even early on, that the all-important New Hampshire contest was going to come down to Clinton or Obama. Despite the closeness between Lou and the Bidens, a campaign endorsement wasn't really seriously considered. The frontrunners were pushing hard for Lou's support and bringing all their resources to bear.

Lou had the opportunity to meet the Obamas a number of times in New Hampshire. He first met the Illinois senator at a house party thrown by a New Hampshire entrepreneur who started a successful yogurt company. The exchanges were polite but rather perfunctory in nature. If there was one audience with the Obamas that made an impression on Lou during the 2008 primary, it occurred at an event held at Manchester's Radisson Hotel. Lou was passing through the hotel lobby when Mrs. Obama approached him. "I was immediately struck by her presence," Lou recalls today. "I was struck by her height and magnetic personality. She was a great advocate for the campaign. She thrust her hand out to shake mine and looked me in the eye. 'Lou. we want you on our team,' she told me. I politely sidestepped any commitment, but I must admit I was intrigued."

In the end, Lou's decision in 2008 had a lot to do with the style of the frontrunners, as well as Mrs. Clinton's most powerful advocate – her husband. Lou thought that Obama was too academic in his approach. "It was just the way he came across to me and it wasn't really the way I saw political engagement," says D'Allesandro. "I didn't have a problem with him; it was in some ways a difficult choice." Years later when Obama was President, Lou had an encounter with him that repainted his 2008 impressions of the man. Lou was at the Manchester Airport with other officials to welcome the president. When Obama deplaned, he worked the reception line, shaking the hands of the assembled dignitaries. When it was Lou's turn to greet the president, Lou mentioned that he had a grandson struggling with a medical condition. He asked the president if he could write something to cheer the boy up. The president continued shaking hands and worked the entire reception line, but then he came back. He brought with him a card with a handwritten note recording well wishes for Lou's grandson, and signed it "Barack Obama." "I was very touched by that," Lou says with a warm smile. "That he would take the time to make the gesture impressed me."

If Presidential star power counted for something in 2008, Hillary Clinton certainly had a secret weapon in her husband. While Bill Clinton was not a visible force in the day-to-day work of the campaign, he was still a former president and the type of guy that could convey the magnetism of the office well. D'Allesandro was getting calls from the former president, and the two men had good, substantial conversations. "Their campaign was behind, as much as 14 points by some polls, but I thought they could win if they were willing to listen to my suggestions," Lou notes. "I know this state and after decades of campaigning in it, I had a pretty good idea of what would work."

That type of give and take was not always the case when presidential campaigns pulled into Manchester. Lou thought back to the prior summer when then-Senator Clinton was in Manchester. In the summer of 2007, Lou and Pat threw a house party for Senator Clinton and more than three hundred guests jammed Lou and Pat's modest-sized, neatly trimmed front lawn. News trucks lined hundreds of feet of their neighborhood streets with their satellite booms extended, and Secret Service agents kept a vigilant eye over the whole affair. Lou observed Clinton work the crowd. "She was in her element; she warmed to the people and they warmed to her. She stayed for hours and didn't want to leave." On the D'Allesandros' refrigerator is a photo of Clinton standing behind Lou and Pat's granddaughter at that party. Clinton's smile beams with an unmistakable and genuine warmth. Lou knew it was that personal contact with the voters that would make the campaign go. The willingness of the Clintons to listen to a local pol and do the grassroots work was impressive by itself, and Lou considered that in making his final decision to endorse her.

In addition to the former president, Lou spent a fair amount of time with the Clinton's daughter Chelsea discussing the campaign's needs. "I felt at ease with the Clintons, and we developed a good rapport," Lou admits. Apparently, the Clintons felt the same way. The campaign needed a boost and Lou had some specific suggestions. He felt that Clinton's efforts in New Hampshire needed a greater authenticity, consistent with what he observed at his home the summer before. "I told Senator Clinton she needed to bring her message directly to the people. It was time to roll up our sleeves and go door-to-door. I took her to my district and we began meeting with voters on their stoops, sitting in their kitchens and face-to-face." Newspapers across the country picked up wire service photos of Clinton and D'Allesandro walking through the New Hampshire snow as they knocked on doors.[4] It wasn't just good optics – it was truly effective campaigning. "She was attentive," Lou observes, "she was a good listener and people warmed to that."

The New Hampshire State Senator and the New York Senator rode a bus to different parts of the state. They sat together and talked strategy. Lou had an abiding conviction that it was working; that the Clinton campaign was gaining on Obama. "I got interviewed by the BBC," Lou recalls. "They wanted to know my observations, what I thought the outcome would be. The whole world was focused on the primary and many people wanted to know whether Clinton could pull it off." Lou confidently predicted a Clinton victory in New Hampshire. It wasn't a "Hail Mary" but the prediction, if realized, would represent a significant political comeback. "I felt the mood," says Lou. "There was an undercurrent of support. The door-to-door effort was producing results. It was resonating with people. Clinton was a very good campaigner in these small meetings. Her message was very genuine."

New Hampshire voters went to the polls on January 8. It was an unusually mild day with temperatures in Manchester reaching 61 degrees. The temperatures were not the only thing elevated that day. Clinton and Obama were in a hot competition for the prize that was a Granite State win. The result was close, but Clinton won and made history too. She bested Obama with a vote of 112,404 to 104,815. It may have been paper-thin but it was nonetheless a win, and a win from behind. In the process, Clinton became the first woman in U.S. history to win a delegate-binding primary. Given the closeness of the popular vote, both Obama and Clinton claimed nine delegates in New Hampshire. Obama was far from out of the running. Edwards tallied 48,699 votes – his campaign was already in trouble.[5]

When the New Hampshire results came in Lou was providing political commentary on WGIR, a Manchester radio station. As it became evident that his bold prediction was about to be proven correct, D'Allesandro left the radio station and rushed to the gymnasium of Southern New Hampshire University where Clinton and her supporters were gathered to usher in the good news. Lou arrived to find a chaotic scene. "On the way over, I was thinking just how amazing of a win it really was. When I got to the gym, it was wall-to-wall jubilation. There was a sense of great accomplishment."

The value of Lou's work in New Hampshire was hard to deny. The Clinton campaign was eager to send D'Allesandro beyond the borders of the Granite State to continue the grassroots progress. Lou was dispatched to Pennsylvania and Ohio. The Ohio primary, scheduled for March 4, came first. Lou spent time campaigning in Cleveland and Youngstown. In Youngstown, Lou met with Sister Kathleen, who managed a convent of Ursuline nuns. The nuns were an industrious group, running a home for juveniles and another for people infected with the AIDS virus. Lou visited the homes and witnessed the nuns' compassion and commitment to social causes. "Those nuns fought so hard to make service to fellow human beings a reality," remembers Lou. "They were wonderful, dynamic ladies. They took me all around Youngstown and we got Hillary's message out in the state's important primary."

When he arrived in Pennsylvania, Lou met a group of football coaches in a smoke-filled Scranton barroom. "It was a large Italian-American community and they must have figured I would fit in pretty comfortably with a group of football coaches from the same ethnic background," Lou laughs. "I met Scranton's mayor, who was a Holy Cross graduate and helped organize a ladies' telephone tree." The tree was a pyramid-organized system for activating a group of people through a series of phone calls. The Pennsylvania phone tree was designed to reach women and according to Lou, it worked very well. "We were in an upper middle-class neighborhood and the host had a large living room in her home," remembers Lou. "They had snacks laid out and women working phones in the living room and other rooms throughout the house. It was all very social and the ladies were having a great time. It was very distinct from a call bank."

When the Pennsylvania vote was cast on April 22, Clinton outpolled Obama 1,273,764 to 1,059,678 and in the process earned 85 delegates in the state, twelve more than Obama.[6] It was a crucial win for Clinton. By the time Pennsylvania cast its vote, Clinton was no longer basking in the glow of a big New Hampshire win but was decidedly behind Obama. Clinton needed a solid win in the Quaker State and she got it. Her husband summed it up: "If she wins a big, big victory in Pennsylvania, I think it'll give her a real boost going into the next primary…I think she's got to win a big victory in Pennsylvania. I think if she does, she can be nominated, but it's up to you."[7] In the end, the Pennsylvania primary may have been more important for what Obama said than either of the Clintons. The Illinois Senator was secretly recorded by the *Huffington Post*. His words resonated in ways he had not intended.

> *You go into these small towns in Pennsylvania and, like a lot of small towns in the Midwest, the jobs have been gone now for 25 years and nothing's replaced them. And they fell through the Clinton administration, and the Bush Administration, and each successive administration has said that somehow these communities are gonna regenerate, and they have not. And it's not surprising when they get bitter, they cling to guns or religion or antipathy to people who aren't like them or anti-immigrant sentiment or anti-trade sentiment as a way to explain their frustrations.*[8]

The Pennsylvania win not only helped boost her campaign, but Obama's remarks were used to cast him as an elitist, something unpopular with working-class whites in states like Ohio and Texas. It was the sort of turning point that kept Clinton in the hunt despite Obama's commanding lead in delegates, and more importantly, in the number of all-important super-delegates.

Clinton was criticized for staying in the race, especially after a rather hard lambasting from Obama. "I was rather taken aback by the demeaning remarks Senator Obama made about people in small-town America," Clinton told the media. "His remarks are elitist and out of touch." A supporter of John Edwards mused, "This is a perfect example of why Democrats lose elections." [9] Clinton backers complained that the party rules were rigged against her and only suspended her campaign after the last primary in June. The drama continued until the August convention in Denver, when Lou and the rest of the delegates nominated Obama by acclamation, but not without Clinton first threatening a push for a roll call vote to illuminate her "18 million cracks" in the glass ceiling of presidential politics. (Clinton was essentially tied with Obama in the Democratic primary popular vote.) [10]

Clinton would get another crack at presidential primary politics, and all of the rules and vagaries of the party. Once again, she would return to New Hampshire. Once again, she would come calling on Lou D'Allesandro.

CHAPTER 18

Lessons from the Campaign Trail

I n the two presidential election cycles that followed 2008, Lou had little to decide. In 2012, Obama was the incumbent president and the presumptive nominee of the Democratic party. With his commanding hold on the electoral process and a clear reelection victory, Obama did not disappoint the party. Four years later, Hillary was back in the Democratic race and Lou's allegiance was essentially decided. But this time Hillary's approach to the New Hampshire primary was far different.

When the 2016 Hillary-for-President effort was organized in the Granite State there was an entirely different feel from 2008. Clinton's New Hampshire State Director was Mike Vlacich, a long-time political operative who ran successful campaigns for a number of state-wide Democratic office holders in New Hampshire.[1] But Vlacich was not the reason for the change. It was something more central than that. According to Lou, "They were running their campaign from New York. They had other plans and were not too interested in what local people had to say."

Lou thought the departure from the grassroots efforts that were responsible for the big comeback win against Obama in 2008 was a big mistake. "It was a question of trust and likeability," Lou observes. "Truly listening to the voters and demonstrating a serious caring for their concerns was what the campaign needed." Instead, there was far less door-to-door and more photo ops with celebrities. "My plan fell on deaf ears," says D'Allesandro. "Catering to the elite was only distancing her from the ordinary voter, the very people she would desperately need in November."

Her competition in the 2016 primary was Vermont Senator Bernie Sanders. The populist Sanders got the jump on Clinton right out of the gate in New Hampshire. "Bernie attacked her right away," Lou observed. "He questioned the money Clinton amassed from speaking fees and what she told some of the audiences, especially the ones in the financial industry." Despite the lack of traction in New Hampshire, Lou was confident that Clinton could win both the nomination and the general election. "I had every confidence in her. She was the experienced candidate and she was competing against what I viewed as a weak Republican field." But as the primary process wore on, Sanders was making inroads, not only with his populist message but also on the character issues he raised from the start. The questions by Bernie were having an impact. It all went to the precise issues Lou thought so important from the earliest days of 2016, trust and likeability.

Clinton's efforts never gathered any momentum in New Hampshire. When Granite State voters went to the polls on February 9, they delivered a resounding win to Sanders. The Vermont senator took every county in the state and won the popular vote by 60% to Clinton's 38 percent. *The New York Times* described the upset as a "harness of working-class fury."[2] Clinton was clearly the establishment candidate with all the advantages afforded by the Democratic Party machinery, but Sanders wasn't going away quietly. New Hampshire made that abundantly clear. When the first-in-the-nation primary was over, there were no trips to other states for D'Allesandro as there had been in 2008. The campaign was organized at the national level and grassroots efforts directed by people like Lou D'Allesandro, folks who were particularly good at pressing the flesh and forging relationships with voters, were not part of the plan. To Lou, "it was all too sterile." The Clinton campaign was long on analytics and modern political tools but short on the type of campaign that built trust one voter at a time. There were other problems as well.

Clinton's campaign was continually plagued by an email scandal and an extraordinary investigation by then-FBI Director James Comey that was probing it. In July, after months of investigations, Comey announced he would not recommend charges against Clinton for running her government emails as Secretary of State through a private email server. Comey did, however, chastise the Secretary of State for the practice.[3] None of it had a good look. Just weeks before Comey made his announcement, Bill Clinton was caught having a meeting with Attorney General Loretta Lynch on an airport tarmac in Phoenix.[4] With the FBI investigation in full swing, the obvious implications were at best a huge distraction. To Lou, "It was just plain stupid. How could he [former President Clinton] think that was a good idea?" There were even questions surrounding the timing of the preparation of Comey's statement. FBI sources revealed it was written in May, two months before the investigation of Hillary Clinton's emails was officially concluded.[5]

The erosion of trust in Hillary wasn't entirely surprising to Lou. The New Hampshire results in February signaled the problem long before Bill Clinton's meeting with Attorney General Lynch or Comey's announcement. Exit polls taken in connection with the nation's first primary highlighted the concern. More voters than not questioned Hillary's honesty, while 91% of the same responders thought Sanders passed the candor test.[6] Lou wasn't shocked by what the results said about Sanders. He also believed that "his [Sanders'] message was on point and resonating." For Lou the question was always whether Bernie was electable, especially in light of Clinton's firm control over the super delegates that helped ensure an establishment candidate's grip on the nomination process. (Super delegates, 714 in number, were appointed by party leadership distinct from the other 4051 delegates that are pledged to candidates during the primary process).[7]

As Clinton did in the 2008 contest with Obama, Sanders competed to the very end. He conceded to Clinton only a few weeks before the Democratic National Convention scheduled for July 25-28 in Philadelphia.[8] As the first female to become the nominee of a major political party, Clinton made history. Even with Sanders out of the way, it didn't take long for new problems to plague the presumptive nominee of the Democratic Party. On July 22, only ten days after Sanders endorsed Clinton while in Portsmouth, New Hampshire, Wikileaks published hacked emails from the Democratic National Committee (DNC) that illuminated the workings of the organization. It was clear that the DNC wasn't neutral in the nomination process. It appeared that the DNC was supporting Clinton and sabotaging the candidacy of Bernie Sanders.[9] Just days before the convention, the news represented another sapping of Clinton's trust with the electorate.

If that weren't bad enough, the Clinton campaign was in for one more big shock before voters went to the polls in November. In what became known as "Comey's October Surprise," the FBI Director announced that he was re-opening the Clinton email investigation as a result of newly discovered emails found on a computer seized during the investigation of disgraced former New York Congressman Anthony Weiner. The Weiner investigation involved online messages of a sexual nature between the Congressman and a teenage girl. The new emails, approximately one-thousand in number, were found on a computer used by both Weiner and his wife Huma Abedin, a top aide to Clinton. The Comey announcement came on Friday, October 28th, just eleven days before the election.[10]

To make matters worse, there was little explanation of how the new probe involved Clinton. *Washington Post* columnist Dana Milbank wrote on the following day,

> *I've long believed in Comey's integrity. But if he doesn't step forward and explain his October surprise, he may inadvertently wind up interfering in the political process – perhaps even reversing the outcome of a presidential election – in a way that would make J. Edgar Hoover gape.*[11]

The October 28th Comey letter that announced the new investigation was retracted on November 6th, two days before the election, after the FBI completed a review of the new emails only to conclude there was nothing new to alter its July conclusion.[12] Polls indicated that Clinton suffered a 17-point drop in net sentiment and Trump an 11-point rise. Scores of political pundits have opined that the actions of the FBI Director cost Clinton the election.[13] If you ask Lou, the seeds of Clinton's defeat were sown long before October 28. "She lost the people's trust," Lou laments. "It's as simple as that. Even more disheartening are the possibilities if the campaign had played to her strengths. She needed to spend more time with the voters and less with the elite. Sanders knew it, and it's why he made it an issue front and center."

To say the outcome of the 2016 election was disheartening to Lou is a colossal understatement. His reaction to Trump is visceral and immediate.

"The man lacks a moral compass," D'Allesandro intones as he shakes his head in disappointment. He looks to the mid-term elections in 2018 with a sense of hope, in part buoyed by doings in his own state. The New Hampshire legislature is comprised of citizen legislators, whose constitutionally-established low pay ensures a certain steady turnover. According to D'Allesandro, "Democrats are being elected to seats that haven't been held by the party in a very long time."

While optimistic, Lou knows the challenge posed by the next presidential election cycle will be significant. Once again, New Hampshire will be in the spotlight in the weeks leading up to the February 2020 primary. Unlike in 2008 and 2016, Lou will face a vetting process with more options. The Democratic field of candidates will be broader and the competition more keen. The stakes for Lou, and Democrats in general, could not be higher as the nation approaches what will be a pivotal election. D'Allesandro, like many on both sides of the aisle, can only imagine what new controversies the Tweeter-in-chief can unleash before the 2020 presidential election season begins in earnest.

While many Americans may yearn for someone other than Donald Trump to lead the country and become the 46th President, the election is not yet the pervasive news topic that it will soon enough become. Nevertheless, Lou is already plugged in to a number of exploratory efforts as plans for 2020 begin to take shape. There have already been phone calls and there are many more to come that D'Allesandro will have to field and evaluate. There are names being bandied about. Some of the more notable include Senator Mark Warner of Virginia; Martin O'Malley, the former governor of Maryland; and Tim Ryan, a Congressman from Ohio. Lou knows there will be others.

As Lou told Mark Liebovich of the *Washington Post* four elections ago, he doesn't take the responsibility lightly. There may be no election in the New Hampshire State Senator's political career where that is truer. While Lou serves his constituents of NH Senate District 20 and Granite Staters from the borders of Massachusetts to Canada, another duty looms, affecting Americans from sea to shining sea. In many ways, 2020 can't come soon enough.

Epilogue

L ou D'Allesandro operates in three political spheres that are sometimes distinct but often overlapping. For more than a generation he has been a vital force in New Hampshire politics and along the way he has also found a unique place as a powerbroker on the national stage. But underpinning all this is the local service he has long provided his constituents. Lou practices a rich and effective brand of retail politics. The stories of Lou pitching in to help friends and neighbors are numerous. There was the case of the young man who was told he had an inoperative neck tumor. His family lost hope when no doctor in New Hampshire had the skills to perform the necessary life-saving operation. Lou drove his neighbor to Mass Eye and Ear, a renowned Boston hospital, where a doctor was found to perform the critical surgery. Thankfully the young man survived his grave illness. Lou has found beds for adolescents suffering from serious mental illnesses, to the relief of worried families. He has helped churches feed the hungry by directing resources to where they were most needed, and he has given countless constituents a hand with a myriad of problems they have faced, large and small.

For Lou, the source of his passion for public service is not a mystery. "We lost Mom when I was still a young boy," Lou laments. "She was the kindest of women who dedicated her life to helping others. Family member or stranger, she quietly went about caring for anyone who needed a helping hand, never expecting accolades or anything in return." As Lou reminisces about his mother, he goes to a deeply emotional place. His eyes soften and water, his voice softens. There is little doubt that he has dedicated much of what he has accomplished to his mother's memory. However brief their years together were, Lou has lived his mother's example well. She would be proud that her son has shared her caring ways and magnified that love over the many years that have passed since her death.

If the source of Lou's desire to serve his neighbor is not difficult to divine, his entry into politics might have been less predictable. Pat remembers Lou addressing a college football rally as the team's captain. "He was a good speaker," notes Mrs. D'Allesandro with a glint in her eye.

"I told him maybe he should go into politics someday." But no matter how much that unsolicited comment may have foretold the future, that was merely an example of two smitten college students kidding each other. What Lou really wanted to do was play professional football. He even secured a tryout with the newly formed Boston Patriots in the American Football League when Coach Lou Saban sent him a letter inviting him to camp. Lou's knee injury interrupted any chance to test his skills on a higher level, and professional football had to be put aside.

His dad's aspirations for Lou were a bit more mundane. D'Allesandro Senior wanted his son to take over his oil burner business. That wasn't in the cards. "I had no interest in that career," says Lou with a conviction that still resonates today. "My brother Paul took it over and did well with it, but it just wasn't for me."

So, Lou took an adventurous spirit, a penchant for sports, and his history degree into the world of education and teaching. The path that ensued was never far away from the next challenge, the next surprise, and if nothing else, anything but boring.

The kid from East Boston became an improbable player on the national political stage; a man about whom Vice President Joe Biden once quipped, "If I was as good a football player as Lou D'Allesandro, I would have been president." He is a citizen legislator with a $100-a-year paycheck about whom then-Senator John Kerry once hoped out loud, "My goal is to get my photo on the refrigerator at the D'Allesandro home."

Lou had many breaks and he lauds his benefactors with effusive praise. He is forever thankful to Senator Warren Rudman, who gave him an early opportunity as the president of Daniel Webster College. Walter Peterson, the former Granite State governor and president of Franklin Pierce University, installed him as a vice president at the school when Lou had to remake himself after his narrow and devastating losses in his two races for Granite State governor. Sister Joseph Landry, a nurse and educator at Rivier College, guided him on the way to a master's degree and became a lifelong friend. But most of all, and most undeniable, is Pat, his wife of 56 years. She has been every bit his partner, not just in raising a family and keeping a home, but in making all of their decisions over the years that required a keen eye and an innate sense of the right direction.

What the kid from East Boston proved is an American story – that all things are possible. Not for a moment has Lou ever believed that American opportunity is a worn-out notion, a cliché. Deep is his faith that leadership, born out of humble service, remains at the core of America's greatness. Lou D'Allesandro's journey proves it, one day, one deed, one election at a time.

~

Acknowledgements

As we began the task of getting this book together, we talked about why, and what was the push to do this? My mother, who left us early, has been remembered by many as someone always wanting to help others. I wanted to explain her influence on me and how this affected my interest in politics. Politics in New Hampshire is unique. This is another window into its workings.

Without my wife's support, nothing would be possible. She is one of a kind. My family has always supported my desire to serve – even when they had to pay a price. They are all part of this adventure.

Mark put it all together and I can't say enough about him. Our effort is here. This is the result.

Lou D'Allesandro

Every book is the product of a great deal of help and support. I owe a debt of gratitude to many who made this effort possible. First and foremost, I must thank Lou and Pat D'Allesandro, not only for trusting me with their story, but for being great historians in interview after interview. Over the past year we have developed a bond of friendship that has made every page, every task a joy to complete. Thank you to my editor, Kate M. Victory Hannisian of Blue Pencil Consulting, and my designer Robin Wrighton, of Wrighton Design. Their expertise and professionalism improved this book greatly. Tom Campbell of King Printing, as always, added much practical advice, and always with great cheer. I appreciate the support of Robert Salvatelli, who read an early draft, and my nephew Jay Vrabec, who contributed to early discussions as the project unfolded. Thank you to Nancy Bell for many helpful discussions as the project developed. Special thanks to Jim Cole, former photographer for the AP. Kevin Grimley of Photografx was an enormous help with arranging and editing graphic images. As always, Linda Pinder lent her support – she is a true friend.

My law office staff, as always, supported a great deal of the effort. Thank you to Gabriella Goodale, Kathleen Welch, Attorney Amanda Mastalerz, and Lizzy Feinberg, and of course, my brother and law partner, David Bodanza. I am blessed to work with David daily and have his counsel and support.

To my wife Adele, children Melissa, Kathryn and Nicholas, and grandson Brody too; thank you for always being there, for understanding and most of all for your unending love and support.

Mark C. Bodanza

Endnotes

Chapter 1

1. Constitution of New Hampshire, Article 25, see *Manual for the General Court*, 2015, No. 64, Published by the Department of State, Gardner, William M., Secretary of State.

2. New Hampshire RSA Chapter 653:9.

3. List of Democratic Party Presidential Primaries, https://en.m.wikipedia.org/wiki/List_of_Democratic_presidential_primaries.

4. New Hampshire RSA Chapter 3:8.

Chapter 2

1. Jim Vrabel, *When In Boston: A Time Line & Almanac* (Boston: Northeastern University Press, 2004), 241.

2. *The Boston Globe*, March 17, 1941.

3. Ibid.

4. New England Historical Society, *When New England Candy Was King: 15 Sweet Facts*, 2016 www.newenglandhistoricalsociety.com/new-england-candy-king-15-sweet-facts.

5. Riverside Military Academy, https://www.cadet.com/AboutUs.

Chapter 3

1. Worcester Academy, https://www.worcesteracademy.org.

2. *A Look Back at New England's Worst Hurricanes, The Boston Globe*, August 31, 2017.

3. Ibid.

4. David Hale, ed., *Towers: Annual of the Class of Nineteen Fifty-Six* (Worcester: The Stobbs Press, Inc., 1956).

5. *The People History*, http://www.thepeoplehistory.com/1955.html.

6. Neal Gabler, *Walt Disney: The Triumph of Imagination* (New York: Vintage Books, 2006), 530-3.

7. Ibid., 520-3.

8. http://www.thepeoplehistory.com/1955.html.

9. *Worcester Telegram*, January 31, 2011.

10. Hale, *Towers: Annual of the Class of Nineteen Fifty-Six* and *1952 NFL Draft*, https://www.pro-football-reference.com/years/1952/draft.html.

11. Hale, *Towers: Annual of the Class of Nineteen Fifty-Six*.

Chapter 4

1. *The New York Times,* March 24, 2010.

2. Michael MacCambridge, *Lamar Hunt: A Life In Sports* (Kansas City: Andrews McMeel Publishing, LLC, 2012), 113.

3. *History Lessons: Big 12, Big 8, SWC,* https://www.espn.com/blog/dallas/colleges/post/_/id/4668611/history-lessons-big-12-8-SWC.

4. https://www.pro-football-reference.com.

5. *1956 Colorado Buffaloes Stats,* https://www.sportseference.com/cfb/schools/Colorado/1956.html.

6. Calvin D. Linton, ed., *The Bicentennial Almanac* (Nashville: Thomas Nelson, Inc., Publishers, 1975), 387.

7. *The People History*, http://www.thepeoplehistory.com/1957.html.

8.   Linton, *The Bicentennial Almanac*, 390.

9.   https://www.JFKibrary.org/Research/Research-Aids/Ready-Reference/JFK-Fast-Facts/Election-1946.aspx.

10.   Linton, *The Bicentennial Almanac*, 393.

11.   https://en.m.wikipedia.org/Frank_Leahy.

Chapter 5

1.   Town of Conway, *Annual Report 1961*, P. 96, digital.unh.edu.

2.   https://en.m.wikipedia.org/wiki/Conway,_New_Hampshire.

3.   *The Boston Globe*, June 1, 2017.

4.   *Atlantic Coast Football League*, https://en.m.wikipedia.org/wiki/Atlantic_Coast_Football_League.

5.   *The Lowell Sun,* May 5, 2016.

6.   *Tom Dempsey's Boot*, https://www.si.com/2014/05/20/afl-history-in-95-objects-tom-dempsey-boot.

7.   https://www.pro-football-reference.com.

8.   https://www.snhu.edu./about-us/leadership-and-history/history.

9.   https://www.snhupenmen.com/information/HallofFame/bios/D-AllesandroLou.

10.   https://www.snhu.edu./about-us/leadership-and-history/history.

11.   https://www.arlingtoncemetery.mil/Explore/Monuments-and-Memorials/President-John-F-Kennedy-Gravesite.

12.   https://en.m.wikipedia.org/Paul_A._Dever.

Chapter 6

1. http://bracknelltowncouncil.gov.uk/bracknell/

2. https://en.m.wikipedia.org/wiki/Hungary_national_basketball_team#Head_coach_position. (1967).

3. https://en.m.wikipedia.org/wiki/Basketball_At_The_Summer_Olympics.

4. https://www.mimoa.eu/projects/Italy/Rome/Palazetto%20dello%sport/.

5. https://www.jfklibrary.org/JFK/JFK-in-History/Alliance-for-progress.aspx.

6. http://www.partners.net/our-legacy.

7. http://www/bbc.com/News/world-latin-America-26713772.

8. Linton, Ed., *The Bicentennial Almanac*, 419.

9. Ibid.

10. Ibid., 420.

Chapter 7

1. Constitution of New Hampshire, Article 9.

2. Ibid., Article 15.

3. https://www.whitehouse.gov/participate/fellows.

4. HB352, "Relative to statewide school food and nutrition programs." (D'Allesandro of Hillsborough, Dist. 34 – To Education.) 1973 House Journal Volume 1, page 252, 2/13/1973.

5. HB3 – "Relative to establishment of a food stamp program and making an appropriation therefore." (D'Allesandro of Hillsborough, Dist 34; Gallen of Grafton Dist. 1; McLane of Merrimack Dist. 16; Sen. Trowbridge of Dist. 11. Let us know if you would like more information about the 1974 bill.

6.   *The New York Times*, April 20, 2001.

7.   https://ballotpedia.org/Nancy_Stiles.

8.   Chapter 170, Laws of 1973, "An Act relative to state-wide school food and nutrition programs." (HB352), 1973 Chapter Laws, page 155-156. Established new paragraph RSA 189:11-a Food and Nutrition Programs.

9.   Public Law 396-79th Congress, June 4, 1946, 60 Stat. 231.

10.   *State of New Hampshire Manual for the General Court*, 2015, No. 64, 182.

11.   *Concord Monitor*, December 9, 2016.

12.   *New Hampshire Union Leader*, November 6, 1974.

13.   *The Washington Post*, April 20, 2001.

14.   Ibid.

15.   *Gay Students Organization at the University of New Hampshire v. Bonner*, 369 F. sup. 1088 (1974).

16.   *The Boston Globe,* July 2, 2007.

17.   *The Nashua Telegraph*, September 6, 2016.

18.   Ibid.

Chapter 8

1.   *New Hampshire Union Leader*, May 7, 1976.

2.   https://en.m.wikipedia.org/wiki/Lake_Balaton.

3.   *New Hampshire Union Leader*, January 12, 2012.

4.   *Concord Monitor*, February 10, 1977.

5.   *New Hampshire Union Leader*, February 6, 1977.

6. *New Hampshire Union Leader*, March 2, 1977.

7. *New Hampshire Union Leader*, March 8, 1977.

8. *New Hampshire Union Leader*, March 29, 1977.

9. "The Clamshell Alliance Holds Nukes At Bay," *Rolling Stone*, July 28, 1977.

10. *The Boston Globe*, April 29, 2009.

11. https://www.ourcampaigns.com/RaceDetail.html?RaceID=174358.

Chapter 9

1. *Concord Monitor*, August 15, 1980.

2. Ibid.

3. Ibid.

4. *Concord Monitor*, August 20, 1980.

5. *Concord Monitor*, August 26, 1980.

6. Ibid.

7. Ibid.

8. *Concord Monitor*, August 27, 1980.

9. *Concord Monitor*, August 28, 1980.

10. *The Nashua Telegraph*, July 8, 1981.

11. *Concord Monitor*, August 29, 1980.

12. https://www.nre.govtrending-rm/doc-collections/fact-sheet/3mile-isle.html.

13. *Portland Press Herald*, August 22, 2015.

14. *Concord Monitor*, September 5, 1980.

15. *State of New Hampshire Manual for the General Court,* 1981, No. 47, 85.

16. *Concord Monitor*, September 16, 1980.

Chapter 10

1.   *Concord Monitor,* August 25, 1982.

2.   Ibid.

3.   *Concord Monitor,* September 9, 1982.

4.   *Concord Monitor,* September 8, 1982.

5.   *Concord Monitor*, August 26, 1987.

6.   Ibid.

7.   https://en.m.wikipedia.org/wiki/United_States_gubernatorial_election_1986.

8.   *Concord Monitor*, August 25, 1982.

9.   *New Hampshire Union Leader*, September 3, 1982.

10. www.pbs.org/wgbh/pages/frontline/shows/clinton/interviews/morris.html.

11. *Concord Monitor*, September 9, 1982.

12. Ibid.

13. Ibid.

14. *Concord Monitor*, September 15, 1982.

15. *Concord Monitor*, September 16, 1982.

16. *The New York Times*, February 22, 2002.

Chapter 11

1. www.nasson.org/history.html.

2. *New Hampshire Union Leader*, April 15, 1986.

3. *New Hampshire Union Leader*, June 19, 1985.

4. *State of New Hampshire Manual for the General Court*, 2015, No. 64, 101.

5. *New Hampshire Union Leader*, April 22, 2001.

6. *New Hampshire Union Leader*, June 2, 2011.

7. www.wmur.com/Article/former-nh-gov.walter-peterson-dies/5168311.

Chapter 12

1. *Sanford News*, November 8, 2007.

2. *New Hampshire Union Leader*, September 10, 1986.

3. *New Hampshire Union Leader*, June 3, 1986.

4. Ibid.

5. *New Hampshire Union Leader*, October 21, 1986.

6. *New Hampshire Union Leader*, October 22, 1986.

7. *New Hampshire Union Leader*, October 26, 1986.

8. *New Hampshire Union Leader*, November 5, 1986.

9. Robert Byrd and Wendy Wolf, *Senate, 1789-1989: Historical Statistics, 1789-1992*, Volume 4 (Washington Government Printing Office, 1993), 285.

10. *New Hampshire Union Leader*, November 6, 1986.

11. Tip O'Neill and Gary Hymet, *All Politics Is Local: And Other Rules of the Game* (Holbrook, MA, Bob Adams, Inc.), 1995, xv.

Chapter 13

1. *New Hampshire Union Leader*, May 28, 1994.

2. *The Boston Sunday Globe*, November 6, 1994.

3. www.nh.electionstats.com/elections/view/585221.

4. www.gencourt.state.nh.us/senate/members/webpages/ district20.aspx.

5. *New Hampshire Union Leader*, May 15, 1998.

6. *New Hampshire Union Leader*, January 21, 1999.

7. *New Hampshire Union Leader*, October 7, 1998.

8. Ibid.

9. Ibid.

10. Ibid.

11. Ibid.

12. https://www.CNN.com/ALLPOLITICS/time/1998/12/21/ livingston.html.

13. www.sos.nh/1998Electioninfo.aspx.

14. *The Nashua Telegraph*, Nov. 5, 1998.

15. Ibid.

16. *New Hampshire Union Leader*, November 4, 1998.

Chapter 14

1. *The Nashua Telegraph*, August 27, 1999.

2. www.fhlboston.com/aboutus/governance/index.jsp.

3. *New Hampshire Union Leader*, November 9, 1994.

4.   www.sos.nh.gov./workarea/DownloadAsset.ASPX?id=3201.

5.   https://www.thenation.com/Article/december-12-2000-in-bush-v-gore-the-supreme-court-gives-the-presidential-election-to-george-w-bush/.

6.   *Bush v. Gore*, 531 U.S. 98 (2001), 128-29.

7.   www.factcheck.org/2008/03/presidents-winning-without-popular-vote/.

8.   https://www.vanityfair.com/news/2004/10/florida.election-2000.

9.   *Marbury v. Madison*, 5 U.S. 137 (1803).

10. www.CNN.com/2013/09/26/us/david-souter-fast-facts/index.html.

11. *Bush v. Gore*, 531 U.S. 98 (2000), 129.

12. Ibid., 135.

13. *State of New Hampshire Manual for the General Court*, 2001, No. 57, 287-292.

14. *New Hampshire Union Leader*, December 7, 2000.

Chapter 15

1.   https://www.nhcf.org/how-can-we-help-you/apply-for-a-grant/carline-cross-fellowships.

2.   *The Daily Journal* (San Mateo, CA), May 1, 2007.

3.   *The Oakland Tribune*, "Requiem for 'Leadfoot Lou,'" May 14, 2007.

4.   *San Francisco Chronicle*, May 1, 2007.

5.   *Serrano v. Priest*, 5 Cal. 3d 584 (1971).

6.   *Jesseman v. State*, No. 82-E-038 (Merrimack County, N.H. Super. Ct. 1982).

7. Augenblick Formula (see RSA 198:27 et seq 1989 & sup. 1999).

8. *Claremont Sch. Dist. v. Governor*, 138 N.H. 183, (1993) (Claremont I).

9. *Claremont Sch. Dist. v. Governor*, 703 Ar 2d. 1353 (N.H. 1997)(Claremont II).

10. http://www.ifda.org/issues/school-funding-constitutional-amendment.

11. Chapter 17, 1999 NH Session Laws.

12. *Concord Monitor*, April 22, 2001.

13. RSA, Section 287-D:6.

14. RSA, Section 287-D:8.

Chapter 16

1. https://uselectionatlas.org/RESULTS/National.php?=2&year=2004&elect=1.

2. Mark Leibovich, *Citizens of the Green Room: Profiles in Courage and Self-Delusion* (Plume, New York) 2014.

3. *The Washington Post,* November 25, 2003.

4. *The Washington Post,* July 28, 2004.

5. www.espn.com/mens-college-basketball/story/_/id/12296176/dean-smith-former-north-carolina-tar-heels-coach-dies-age-83.

6. *The Washington Post,* December 7, 2003.

7. https://en.m.wikipedia.org/wiki/United_States_presidential_election_in-new_hamsphire,_2004.

8. *The New York Times*, August 8, 2008.

9. *The New York Times*, November 5, 2004.

10. *The New York Times*, December 7, 2010.

11. *The New York Times*, January 20, 2008.

12. William McDonald, The New York Times, The Obits 2012 (Workman Publishing, New York) 2011, 198.

13. *The Washington Post*, December 7, 2003.

Chapter 17

1. https://www.billrichards.com/about-bill/biography.

2. *The New York Times*, May 30, 2015.

3. *The New York Times*, December 19, 1972.

4. *Concord Monitor*, December 16, 2007.

5. https://en.m.wikipedia.org/wiki/New_Hampshire_ Democratic_primary,_2008.

6. https://en.m.wikipedia.org/wiki/Pennsylvania_ Democratic_primary,_2008.

7. Ibid.

8. https://www.thenation.com/article/the-2008- democratic-primary-was-far-nastier-than-2016s/.

9. Ibid.

10. https://en.m.wikipedia.org/wiki/2008_ Democratic_National_Convention.

Chapter 18

1. *The Boston Globe*, March 26, 2015.

2. *The New York Times*, February 9, 2016.

3. *The New York Times*, April 22, 2017.

4. *The San Diego Union-Tribune*, August 17, 2017.

5. *Newsweek*, August 31, 2017.

6. *The Wall Street Journal*, February 9, 2016.

7. *Huffington Post*, May 23, 2016.

8. *The Washington Post*, July 12, 2016.

9. *The Washington Post*, July 22, 2016.

10. *The Washington Post*, October 29, 2016.

11. Ibid.

12. *The New York Times*, November 6, 2016.

13. https://www.alternet.org/election-2016/fbi-director-james-comeys-october-doomed-hillary-clintons-candidacy-analysis.